40 DAYS OF POWER

Books By T.D. Jakes

40 Days of Power

Help Me, I've Fallen and I Can't Get Up!

Hope for Every Moment

Insights to Help You Survive Peaks and Valleys

It's Time to Reveal What God Longs to Heal

Power for Living

Release Your Anointing

The Harvest

Water in the Wilderness

Woman, Thou Art Loosed!

Why? Because You're Anointed!

40 DAYS OF POWER

T.D. JAKES

Compiled by Angela Rickabaugh Shears.

DESTINY IMAGE® PUBLISHERS, INC.
P.O. Box 310, Shippensburg, PA 17257-0310

"Speaking to the Purposes of God for This Generation and for the Generations to Come."

This book and all other Destiny Image, Revival Press, Mercy Place, Fresh Bread, Destiny Image Fiction, and Treasure House books are available at Christian bookstores and distributors worldwide.
For a U.S. bookstore nearest you, call 1-800-722-6774.
For more information on foreign distributors, call 717-532-3040.
Reach us on the Internet: www.destinyimage.com.

Previously Published ISBN 13: 978-0-7684-2840-7

ISBN 13: 978-0-7684-4229-8

For Worldwide Distribution, Printed in the U.S.A.

1 2 3 4 5 6 7 8 9 10 11 / 18 17 16 15 14 13

CONTENTS

DAY 1

PURPOSE AND POWER

And we know that all things work together for good to them that love God, to them who are the called according to His purpose (Romans 8:28).

REFLECTION

When we look at the course of our lives, it sometimes appears to be a chaotic path. The course seems to have no certain direction. Yes, even Christians often find themselves questioning the meaning and course of their lives. The things that God does in our lives and the incidents and situations that happen in many instances appear to be a haphazard, erratic display of a madman who gets pleasure from seeing his subjects suffer and live in despair.

But with God, this is not the case. There is a reason to the riddle. There is an answer to the question, clarity to the confusion, and calmness in the chaos. A bright new day dawns after the dark night. There is a time and a purpose to everything under the sun, a method to the madness.

(POWER FOR LIVING, Chapter 1)

POWER LIVING PERSPECTIVE

1. Does your life have direction? Why or why not? What steps can you take to turn life's chaos into a calm and divinely directed path to your destiny?

   It seemed to have direction but my plans are being wrecked to be replaced by God's. So, yes, I'm following God's direction. I must trust God, obtain assurance in my purpose, don't worry about what others' think, and rest in knowing that all things are working together for my good & God's know's my end.

2. Knowing God's divine purpose for your life helps you understand and make sense of the chaos. People who possess such knowledge possess power. Do you know God's divine purpose for your life? Actively seeking His will gives you power. List ways you can seek His divine purpose for your life.

   Yes, God has revealed unto me His purpose for my life.
   - Keep seeking Him
   - Trust Him & His plan

3. When people sought to kill Jesus for His stand and boldness in declaring the truth, He didn't get fearful and back down—Jesus stood His ground. When you know your divine purpose, you have the power to stand your ground. Think of issues of truth about which you will stand your ground—no matter what.

I'm following God's lead even if people talk about me because they don't understand. I'm forsaking my plans & everyone else's plans for God's. He knows what's best. He's preparing me, and He won't put more on me than I can bear. He's also going to make everyone & everything bow in submission of understanding to Him & His plan for my life.

4. When you are assured of your purpose, you're not fearful of men or external personal conflicts that attempt to hinder you. Do you have the confidence to boldly stand for God alone? If not, why?

YES! It was something I had to learn and now that I know, I'm not turning back, nor am I worried about people understanding (or lack thereof). I'll go if I have to go by myself.

5. When you know your purpose, you won't sit and passively allow things to occur in your life that are contrary to God's purpose and vision. How can you start living today knowing you have the power to fulfill your purpose? What changes will you make in your attitude?

Meditation

He who sins is of the devil, for the devil has sinned from the beginning. For this purpose the Son of God was manifested, that He might destroy the works of the devil (1 John 3:8 NKJV).

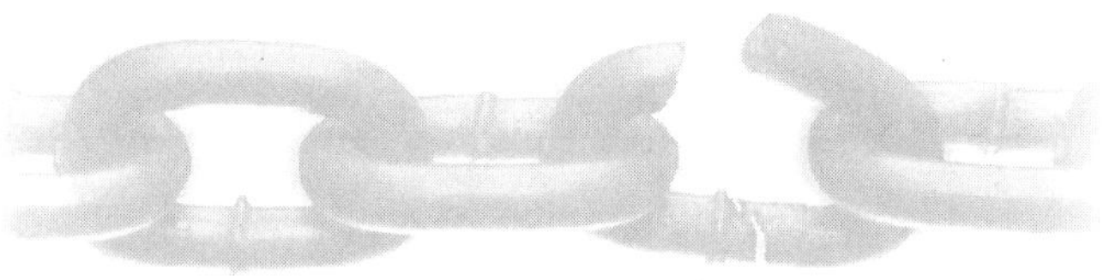

Knowing God's divine purpose for your life is one of the greatest assets and enablements to help make sense of the perplexities and complications that sometimes overwhelm. People who possess such knowledge possess power.

DAY 2

Your Help Comes From the Lord

My help comes from the Lord, who made heaven and earth (Psalm 121:2 NKJV).

REFLECTION

Therefore, if you are confused, ready to give up, wondering what's going on and what all the turmoil and chaos you're experiencing is about, ask God, "Why?" He just might say, "It's purpose." Maybe He's building a foundation of character in your life. Perhaps it will enable you to obtain the success and blessing that is to be poured into your life. Maybe it is a prelude to the powerful anointing that is about to come upon you.

He's got to teach you how to trust Him now, while you are in the desert, so that when you get into the Promised Land and people start acting funny toward you because they're jealous of the anointing on your life, you won't be afraid to cut ungodly ties. You know your help comes not from others but from the Lord. Do you understand what I'm saying? I know you do. If you don't, you'd better ask somebody! But don't just ask anybody, ask the Lord! Call on the Lord and He will answer you. Go ahead. Don't be afraid. Ask Him, "Lord, *why?*"

(POWER FOR LIVING, Chapter 1)

Power Living Perspective

1. Do you sometimes think that God has built enough "character," and you'd rather not have to go through any more tough times? Write a letter to God explaining these feelings. He will appreciate your honesty and respect.

2. Do you trust God completely? How about times when your health isn't 100 percent, your job is in jeopardy, your family is facing financial or emotional problems? Trust Him especially during these times. He will never leave you nor forsake you. Never. List a time when you realized God was with you all the way through a difficult circumstance.

When I quit my job. He's been supplying my every need. I don't have to worry because He always steps in right on time. He's faithful, He's merciful & gracious!

3. Do you feel comfortable enough in your relationship with God to ask Him, "Why?" What do you think His reaction will be if you ask Him why certain things have happened to you? Is this the reaction of a loving and forgiving God?

His reaction will be gentle and caring and bringing a sense of peace & assurance that He is God! Yes, indeed!

4. You are destined, purposed, and called to do something great in life! It is unique to your personality, to your life experiences, to your sphere of influence, and so dependent on your color, culture, needs, failures, and shortcomings that nobody but you can claim it. Believe this! Act on it! What will you do today to claim your destiny?

I will seek God to help me do the things that cause me to be fulfilled in Him. To trust Him completely even when I don't understand or see the way.

5. God wants to use you for His master plan. Are you available? Are you willing to put His desires first in your life? Explain how your life will change if you allow His power for living to overcome all your troubling circumstances.

There's a peace when you surrender your all to God. It's a new level of growth, maturity, and trust. You realize that He's always faithful to come through and life starts to make so much more sense.

MEDITATION

For though He was crucified in weakness, yet He lives by the ***power of God****. For we also are weak in Him, but we shall live with Him by the* ***power of God****...* (2 Corinthians 13:4 NKJV).

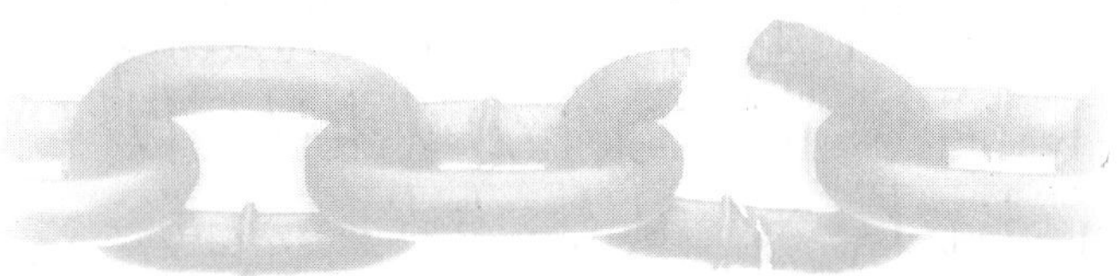

You are a man or woman of destiny. There is a purpose and reason for your life. You are going through so much because you were not brought into this earth haphazardly, but because there is actually some divine, ordained logic to your being. You are not some mistake your mother and father made one night in the heat of passion or uncontrollable lust. Claim this truth today.

DAY 3

GOD'S PURPOSE WILL STAND

Remember the former things, those of long ago; I am God, and there is no other; I am God, and there is none like Me. I make known the end from the beginning, from ancient times, what is still to come. I say: My purpose will stand, and I will do all that I please (Isaiah 46:9-10 NIV).

REFLECTION

Wait a minute, God said He is declaring the end from the beginning. That's backward. That's out of sequence. That's out of order. You never declare the end from the beginning. Anybody who tells a good joke will tell you not to tell the punch line before the introduction. But God says, "I'll do it backward for you. I declare the end from the beginning. I don't start at the foundation. I reverse the order. I start with the end of it, then I go back and start working on the beginning and make the beginning work into the end." God says, "I establish purpose and then I build procedure."

God says, "I put the victory in the heavenlies, then I start from the earth and move upward. I make sure everything is set according to My design, then I work it out according to My purpose and My plan, My will and My way." That's why God is not nervous when you are nervous because He has set your end from the beginning. While you're struggling, groping, and growling, trying to get it together, and wondering whether you will make it, God knows you're going make it, because He has already set your end!

(POWER FOR LIVING, Chapter 1)

Power Living Perspective

1. God says, "I establish purpose and then I build procedure." Because God knows the end from the beginning, how does that give you comfort when realizing your potential and purpose?

2. After you determine God's purpose for your life, do you believe that He will give you the power to achieve that purpose? How can you draw on that power to forge ahead?

3. How does "struggling, groping, and growling, trying to get it together, and wondering whether you will make it" limit the power God anoints you with to overcome?

4. God *knows* you are going to make it through whatever trial and troubles you have at the moment. Write about a time when you were sure you couldn't get through it. Thank Him for His faithfulness.

5. Was there ever a time when you read the last page of a book to see how it turned out? Did you ever fast-forward a movie to see what happened in the end? God created your beginning, and He already wrote your finale. Now He is crafting exciting and rewarding middle scenes. How will submitting your will to Him today affect the ending?

MEDITATION

The end of a thing is better than its beginning; the patient in spirit is better than the proud in spirit (Ecclesiastes 7:8 NKJV).

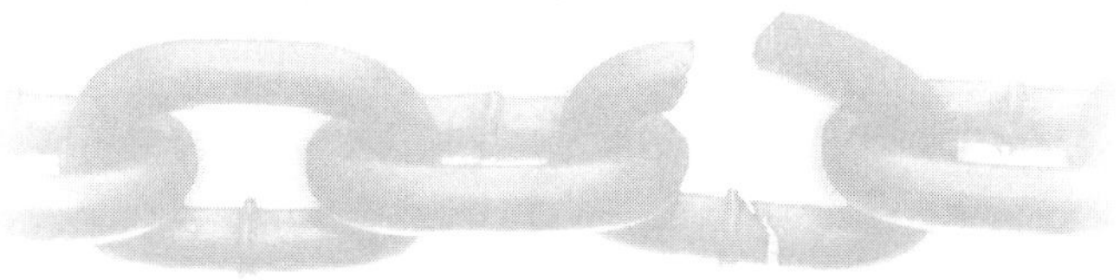

Placing trust in the Lord for the end of our lives takes the pressure and stress off the daily duties of life. Allow yourself to be comforted knowing that He is in total control of the past, present, and future.

DAY

4

BUILD A HOUSE OF GLORY

Now therefore ye are no more strangers and foreigners, but fellowcitizens with the saints, and of the household of God; and are built upon the foundation of the apostles and prophets, Jesus Christ Himself being the chief corner stone; in whom all the building fitly framed together groweth unto an holy temple in the Lord: in whom ye also are builded together for a habitation of God through the Spirit (Ephesians 2:19-22).

REFLECTION

God's approach to destiny is first establishing the purpose, then reverting to the beginning to develop you and instruct you on how to fulfill the purpose. God works out purpose the way you would design and construct a house. If you wanted to build a massive house, you must first hire an architect. The architect takes the vision you have for the house and transforms it onto paper (blueprint), establishing what it shall be before it is ever built. Then the carpenter comes in and makes the vision a reality by constructing in material form (manifesting in the present) the design (vision) that the architect has established on paper (the blueprint).

I want you to know that God is the Master Architect (designer) and Master Builder all in one. He never gets confused about what is planned or how it is to be built. When God builds something, He builds it for maximum efficiency and optimal performance. We get confused and doubt the outcome. Discouraged, we often find ourselves asking God, "Why did You make me wait while other people went forth? Why does it take so long for my breakthrough to come?" God responds, "What does the blueprint say? What do the specifications call for?"

(POWER FOR LIVING, Chapter 1)

Power Living Perspective

1. God first establishes your purpose, then reverts to the beginning to develop you and instruct you on how to fulfill the purpose. Are you allowing Him to develop and instruct you? Why is it so hard to give Him full reins to direct your path?

2. God is never confused about what is planned or how it is to be built. When He builds something, He builds it for maximum efficiency and optimal performance. Too often we feel like we have no energy or effectiveness. What are some ways you can plug back into the Power Source and boost your performance?

3. When God says, "I'm building a solid foundation so you'll better understand pressure and be able to go through the storms of life without being moved or shaken," can you accept that principle without too much rebellion?

4. Do you believe that "Anything that is worth having is worth fighting for and worth working hard for"? List a few things that you believe are worth fighting for and worth working hard for.

5. "God is building a house of glory, a house filled with His Spirit, governed by His Word (will), and submitted to the lordship of His Son, Jesus Christ. As tenants of that house, we are called to represent the Builder and Lord of that house by manifesting His glory on the earth." Explain what this means to you.

MEDITATION

But we have this treasure in earthen vessels, that the excellency of the power may be of God, and not of us (2 Corinthians 4:7).

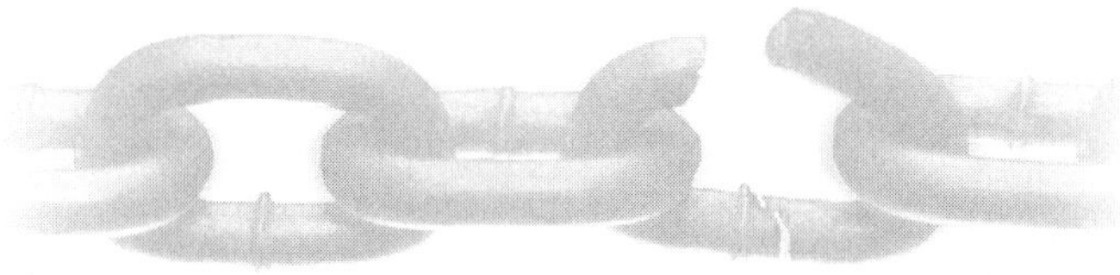

Are you ready to accept the "excellency of the power" of God in your life?

DAY 5

THE POWER OF WHY

How long, O Lord, must I call for help, but You do not listen? Or cry out to You, "Violence!" but You do not save? Why do You make me look at injustice? Why do You tolerate wrong? Destruction and violence are before me; there is strife, and conflict abounds. Therefore the law is paralyzed, and justice never prevails. The wicked hem in the righteous, so that justice is perverted.... Your eyes are too pure to look on evil; You cannot tolerate wrong. Why then do You tolerate the treacherous? Why are You silent while the wicked swallow up those more righteous than themselves? (Habakkuk 1:2-4,13 NIV)

REFLECTION

Have you been asking God questions about your life and the society in which you live? Why so much heartache, so much pain? Have you, like the prophet Habakkuk, become perplexed, distraught, saddened, grieved, and even angered at the injustices of today? What about the plight of the poor, the pain of the oppressed, the continual wickedness of humankind, and the hypocrisy and complacency of the Church? Have you cried in the midnight hour and asked God, "How long?" Have you thought, like Habakkuk, that maybe God just was not listening?

Are there problems in your life left unresolved, questions unanswered? Have you considered entering into the courtroom of the Kingdom of God to ask, "God, Your Honor, *why?* What's going on? What is the purpose? What's happening in my life?"

(POWER FOR LIVING, Chapter 2)

Power Living Perspective

1. Asking why is not necessarily a rebellious attempt to question God's authority. Hearing God's answer to your question will empower you to become all that He destined you to be. Are you afraid of His answer? Why?

2. "God, I want to draw from Your spiritual and intellectual resources until Your thoughts become my thoughts, and Your ways become my ways, and Your ideas become my ideas." Do you want a supernatural exchange with God? What do you anticipate this exchange to be like?

3. "God, I'm not questioning Your right or ability to rule or govern, but show me the strategy. Show me Your plan and purpose for my life." Pray until you are sure that He has given you His plan and purpose. Write what He has revealed to you.

4. "Every now and then, tell me and remind me how it's going to end!" Sometimes *His* plans get nudged aside by *our* plans. Be watchful and listen for signs that you are offtrack. Allow the Holy Spirit to steer you back onto destiny's path. List ways you could get sidetracked.

5. "Lord, I need a breakthrough right now—not tomorrow, not next week, next month, or next year. Lord, I need it now!" Why is it so important to turn to God and ask why rather than turning to friends or an old bad habit?

MEDITATION

***Why** do the heathen rage, and the people imagine a vain thing? The kings of the earth set themselves, and the rulers take counsel together, against the Lord, and against His anointed...* (Psalm 2:1-2).

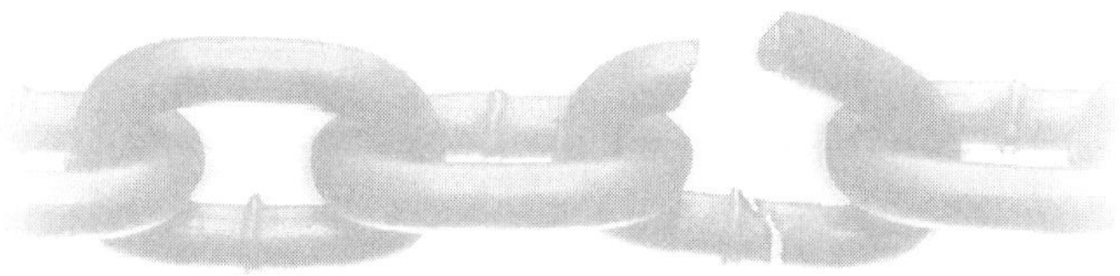

Even the psalmist asked why. Does this give you hope and solace?

DAY 6

COMMUNICATE WITH ME

And let us arise, and go up to Bethel; and I will make there an altar unto God, who answered me in the day of my distress, and was with me in the way which I went (Genesis 35:3).

REFLECTION

If I ask you, "Why?" I'm not merely saying, "Give me an answer." It's a demand, an inquiry, a request that you talk with me, that you dialogue with me until I understand your thought process. It says, "Communicate with me until I understand your wisdom, until I know how to deduce for myself and determine in my mind the things that you have deciphered in your maturity. I know that I may appear to be inferior and my intellect may be less developed than yours, but explain the situation and break it down to my level of understanding that I might be able to determine the matter for myself. That way, when you're not around, I can equate and come to a solution or conclusion on my own without the help of others. I need to think in a decisive manner for myself that I may learn to be independent."

(POWER FOR LIVING, Chapter 2)

POWER LIVING PERSPECTIVE

1. Would you rather be given the answers to questions from a person you admire—or would you rather sit down and talk with the person, get to know how they think, enjoy the conversation, and develop a relationship with that person? Name someone you admire and would like to get to know. Now write a plan of action to contact the person and make it happen!

2. Jesus is the ultimate Person all believers should want to know better. Write a plan of action to make it happen!

3. "I need to think in a decisive manner for myself that I may learn to be independent." Our dependence needs to be on God only. If you are depending on yourself, others, other things, the future, or the past, you *will* be disappointed. List a few ways you can become more independent and more dependent on Jesus.

____

____

____

____

____

____

4. "I thought, *I don't want to spend all of my life trying to figure out what life's really all about, and by the time I finally realize what's actually going on, it's time to go*." Have you ever considered this thought? How does it change the way you look at the future?

____

____

____

____

____

____

5. "God, give me the divine philosophy, the heavenly strategy, and the majestic plan. I want to know what it's really all about. Please God, answer the why of the matter." You can have peace of mind about "the matter" by:

MEDITATION

For I know the thoughts that I think toward you, saith the Lord, thoughts of peace, and not of evil, to give you an expected end (Jeremiah 29:11).

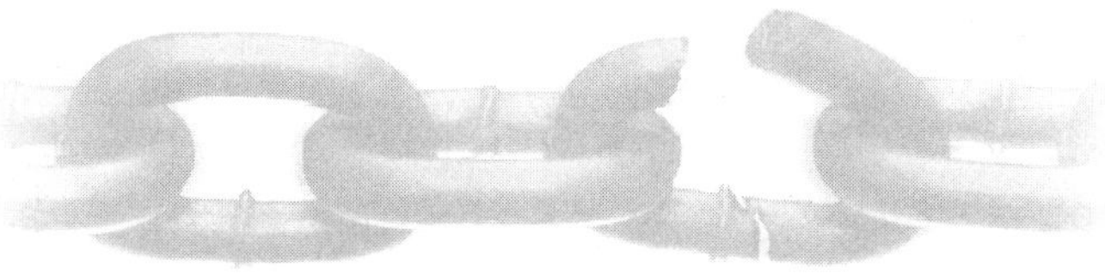

God knows our beginning, middle, and ending. Communicate with Him about each step along the way.

DAY 7

LIFE IS A TALE TOLD BY A FOOL?

The fear of the Lord is the beginning of knowledge, but fools despise wisdom and instruction (Proverbs 1:7 NKJV).

REFLECTION

Shakespeare wrote, "Life is a tale told by an idiot." He said not to ask why, because there is no answer. Life, according to Dickens, is just a bombardment of separated incidents that have no harmony, relativity, or relationship with one another. It's just this, that, and the other. In life there is no formation, no conclusion, no answer—just a wild man telling a strange story that has no ending, solution, or equation. Life is sporadic, out of control, wild, crazy, and all mixed up. Don't try to figure it out. Just leave it where it is. Don't worry about it. Just lay it down to the side. Don't try to understand anything about what life is really all about.

The question that needs to be answered is, "Why are all the fatalists and misguided doomsayers of the world wrong?" We are seeking to address this dilemma of why the anointed person experiences joy and pain, suffering and comfort, tragedy and triumph. This is the same anointing that gives the believer power for living.

(Power for Living, CHAPTER 2)

Power Living Perspective

1. "Life, according to Dickens, is just a bombardment of separated incidents that have no harmony, relativity, or relationship with one another." Some religions agree with this concept of life. How is this contrary to Christian truth? Write a few instances when you realized that one seemingly unrelated incident was actually fully connected to another through the Lord's plan.

2. "Life is sporadic, out of control, wild, crazy, and all mixed up. Don't try to figure it out." Can you think of incidents in the Bible when something prophesied centuries previously came to pass? Write about a few.

3. "The biblical, godly perspective of life is one of insight, direction, hope, fulfilled dreams, and visions." Search the Bible and write at least five instances where God's children are urged to seek wisdom, ask for direction, embrace hope, dream dreams, and see visions.

4. "Just because the vision tarries doesn't mean God has changed His mind or given up on you." It is so easy to get discouraged and lose sight of His plan. What can you do when you feel as if life is being told by a fool?

5. It could be that the timing or the situation is not right for God to get the ultimate glory and benefit out of your trusting in Him. When these times come, rely on your faith in a faithful God. How can you put action to these words?

MEDITATION

No temptation has overtaken you except such as is common to man; but God is faithful, who will not allow you to be tempted beyond what you are able, but with the temptation will also make the way of escape, that you may be able to bear it (1 Corinthians 10:13 NKJV).

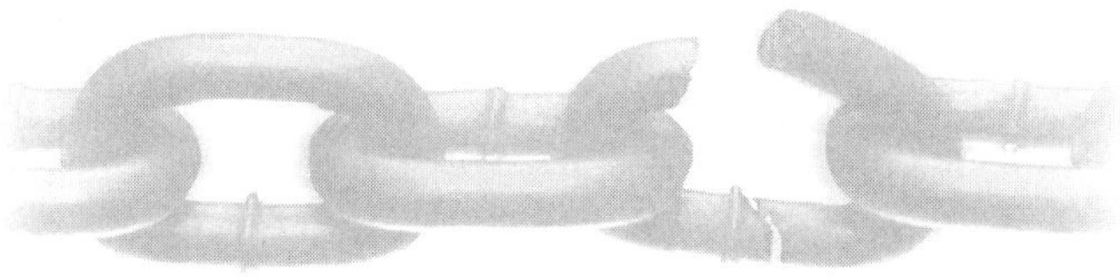

Your life's tale is told by a faithful and merciful God who loves you now and forever.

DAY 8

POWER TO SEEK AND FIND

If any of you lacks wisdom, let him ask of God, who gives to all liberally and without reproach, and it will be given to him (James 1:5 NKJV).

REFLECTION

I was taught not to ask God, "Why?" I was taught that true Christians never ask God why. It was considered a breech of our faith to ask God *why*. If you really believe God, you just completely accept everything that comes your way without asking God anything pertaining to its reason for happening—as if God gets insulted, mad, or feels like you're questioning His authority when you ask Him why. Others feel that if you ask why God is intimidated by your quest for knowledge, or that you might ask Him something that He cannot answer, or that you might offend or hinder God's ability to be omniscient. For whatever the reason, many feel that they should not ask why of Almighty God.

However, God says, "Come to Me and ask Me why." He says, "I'm not afraid of your questions. I'm not afraid of you." God is not insecure in His sovereignty. He's not envious of us or afraid that His position, power, or authority is going to be jeopardized by you or anybody else knowing too much. I don't care how many times you have to ask Him. He says ask of Him who gives freely as He wills. God said, "When you are confused, your mind is perplexed, your heart is troubled, and you don't know what in the world to do, come to Me and ask Me."

(POWER FOR LIVING, Chapter 3)

POWER LIVING PERSPECTIVE

1. Were you taught not to ask God why? Do you think the reasoning is valid? Why or why not?

2. Do you think God gets angry or insulted if you ask Him why? What does that say about your relationship with him?

3. Write James 1:5 in your own words. How does this verse contradict those who say you are not to question God?

4. "When you are confused, your mind is perplexed, your heart is troubled, and you don't know what in the world to do, come to Me and ask Me." Do you believe this? What will you ask Him about today?

5. Because God has anointed you with power to seek and find the mysteries of life, how will you use this power to become more like Jesus?

MEDITATION

I love those who love Me, and those who seek Me diligently will find Me (Proverbs 8:17 NKJV).

And you will seek Me and find Me, when you search for Me with all your heart (Jeremiah 29:13 NKJV).

For everyone who asks receives, and he who seeks finds, and to him who knocks it will be opened (Matthew 7:8 NKJV).

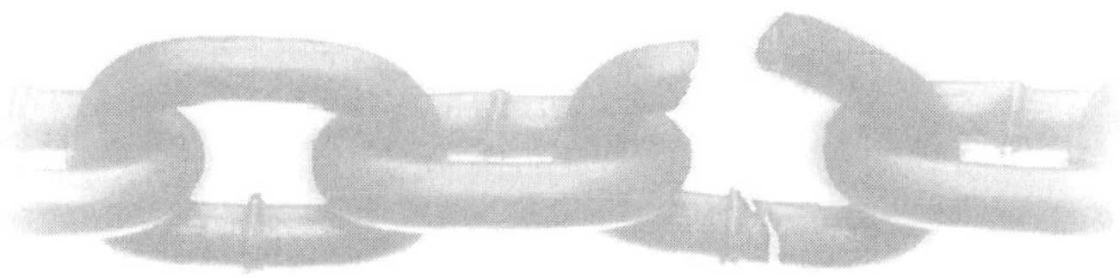

There are many other Scriptures that declare God's desire for you to find Him.

Seek Him every day in every way.

DAY

9

POWER IN PERSPECTIVE

And He spake a parable unto them to this end, that men ought always to pray, and not to faint; saying, "There was in a city a judge, which feared not God, neither regarded man: and there was a widow in that city; and she came unto him, saying, 'Avenge me of mine adversary.' And he would not for awhile: but afterward he said within himself, 'Though I fear not God, nor regard man; yet because this widow troubleth me, I will avenge her, lest by her continual coming she weary me.'" And the Lord said, "Hear what the unjust judge saith. And shall not God avenge His own elect, which cry day and night unto Him, though He bear long with them? I tell you that He will avenge them speedily. Nevertheless when the Son of Man cometh, shall He find faith on the earth?" (Luke 18:1-8).

REFLECTION

The judge did not want to hear the woman's plea for justice, but the woman pressed him so hard and so long that he granted the woman's request. The judge did this not because he felt sorry for her or had compassion on her, but the judge granted her petition simply because the lady literally "got on his nerves." The widow, realizing the judge's reluctance and refusal to hear her, could have lost hope, lost faith, and simply given up. But the woman was persistent, and her persistence was actually fueled and empowered by her faith—a faith that declares, "I don't care how long it takes; I don't care what I have to suffer or what pain I must endure; I don't care who doesn't agree with me or doesn't like me for believing God; I know that if I keep on keeping on, one day, sooner or later, my change is going to come and I will see the salvation of the Lord."

Regardless of the excesses and some erroneous teachings that have been associated with the "Word of Faith" and Charismatic movements, Christians must forever remember and be mindful of the fact that the Word of God declares that anything in our lives that is not rooted in or brought about by faith in the Almighty is sin. For without faith it is impossible to please God.

(POWER FOR LIVING, Chapter 3)

POWER LIVING PERSPECTIVE

1. The woman in the parable had such power of persistence that the judge finally gave in. Think of a time when you gave up before accomplishing your goal. Write about it. Then write what you could have done differently.

2. "The widow, realizing the judge's reluctance and refusal to hear her, could have lost hope, lost faith, and simply given up." Do you resist the urge to be one of "those" people who don't take *no* for an answer? Do you shy away from being the "squeaky wheel"? What does this parable tell you about those attitudes?

3. Does *your* faith declare: "I don't care how long it takes; I don't care what I have to suffer or what pain I must endure; I don't care who doesn't agree with me or doesn't like me for believing God; I know that if I keep on keeping on, one day, sooner or later, my change is going to come and I will see the salvation of the Lord"? Why or why not?

4. Faith for the believer is what gasoline is for an automobile; it's what electricity is for lights and high-powered appliances. List five more comparisons.

5. "Faith in God and confidence in self fuels our lives and gives motivation, inspiration, and eternal hope." How confident are you in this statement?

MEDITATION

For in it the righteousness of God is revealed from faith to faith; as it is written, "The just shall live by faith" (Romans 1:17 NKJV).

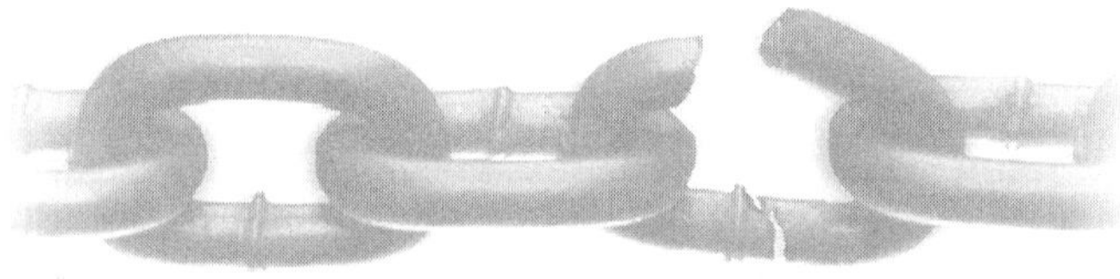

Faith is the foundation of your life in Christ.

Are you planted on a firm foundation of faith and persistence?

DAY

10

Charismatic Witchcraft

For it is God who works in you both to will and to do for His good pleasure (Philippians 2:13 NKJV).

REFLECTION

Please, let me be clear on what faith is, so that you make no mistakes about what I'm talking about. I'm not talking about some kind of feel-good confession rooted in humanism, saying, "I'm OK, you're OK." Nor am I referring to some kind of manipulation of Scripture to formulate my recipe for success. That's a form of Charismatic witchcraft, and I don't associate with witches. No! When I say *faith*, I'm talking about complete, absolute, uncompromising trust in God. It is a faith that knows my successes in life are not because of some great wonderful ability of my own, but my help comes from the Lord (see Ps. 40:17). For He, the Lord God Almighty, enables me to do His good will and all things for His good pleasure (see Phil. 2:13).

It is God who works all things and does all things together for our good. In accordance with His calling on our lives and His overall purpose for humankind, He does these things (trials as well as blessings) as prerequisites of our love for Him. Love directed toward God is reflected and expressed by our obedience to His Word and submission to His commands (see 1 John 5:2-3). We must know that the supreme principle of faith is the product of God's love toward us. "Faith...worketh by love" (Gal. 5:6).

(POWER FOR LIVING, Chapter 3)

POWER LIVING PERSPECTIVE

1. Do you know someone who manipulates Scripture to suit his or her needs or a congregation's needs? How is this like Charismatic witchcraft?

2. "We must know that the supreme principle of faith is the product of God's love toward us." Describe God's love for you in detail. Believe that He loves you beyond your comprehension.

3. God's *agape* love means that your welfare is always His number one concern. Your heavenly Father, the One who loved you while you were yet a sinner, unworthy of love, will never leave you nor forsake you. Think about a time when someone you loved disappointed you or left you. Write how very different God's love for you is.

4. "...Christians are far too impatient. If God doesn't speak in the first five minutes of our prayer time, we get up, shake ourselves off, and concede that God is not talking today. We no longer have the kind of tenacity, diligence, and persistence like the saints of old." Do you agree with these statements? Why or why not?

5. "If God has spoken to you about your life and has shown you a glorious end to the matter, wait on it. If, in your waiting, you exercise faith, prayer, and patience, the vision shall surely come to pass." List ways you can exercise faith, prayer, and patience while you wait for God's perfect answer.

MEDITATION

My brethren, count it all joy when you fall into various trials, knowing that the testing of your faith produces patience. But let patience have its perfect work, that you may be perfect and complete, lacking nothing (James 1:2-4 NKJV).

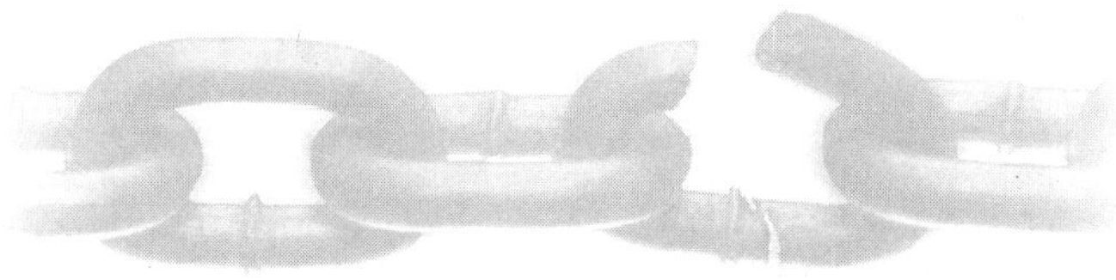

Do you feel "perfect and complete, lacking nothing"?

Faith in God's unfailing love will give you that comfort.

DAY

11

SPIRIT POWER

But the anointing [power] *which you have received from Him abides in you, and you do not need that anyone teach you; but as the same anointing teaches you concerning all things, and is true, and is not a lie, and just as it has taught you, you will abide in Him* (1 John 2:27 NKJV).

REFLECTION

Teachers who successfully educate not only must establish and maintain a dialogue with the students, but also must adequately and competently answer complex, difficult, and perplexing questions in the minds of students. From that point, the interaction between students and teacher conveys the message that says, "I respect your ability as a teacher to be able to give me answers." At this stage in the educational process, trust begins. If the teacher has proven continually that he or she has the students' personal, as well as academic, interest in mind, the learning process advances to the pivotal and the most warranted stage referred to as discipleship.

From that point on, the student communicates to the teacher that through their relationship he wants an exchange. Not only an exchange of answers, but for the teacher to teach him how to reason like a teacher. Therefore, this exchange will enable the student to become a teacher and ultimately teach other people. This is what God really desires and wishes to share with us as disciples of Christ.

(POWER FOR LIVING, Chapter 4)

POWER LIVING PERSPECTIVE

1. What is your first thought when someone mentions *teacher* or *school?* Is it a pleasant thought—or unpleasant? Why?

2. Did you have a good relationship with most of your teachers in school? If you had it to do over, would you ask more questions, do extra credit work, or stay after class to get more help in a tough subject?

3. How can you improve the relationship you have with *the* Teacher? Are you willing to "stay after" to gain as much wisdom as possible from Him?

4. The power for living comes from knowledge of God and His ways. Are you a student willing to study His Word and obey His commandments? What will the end result be?

5. "God wants to communicate with us, which is one of the primary reasons He sent the Holy Spirit to commune with us—so we might learn something of His ways and purposes." How would you rate your communication skills with God? Is there room for improvement?

MEDITATION

That we henceforth be no more children, tossed to and fro, and carried about with every wind of doctrine, by the sleight of men, and cunning craftiness, whereby they lie in wait to deceive; but speaking the truth in love, may grow up into Him in all things, which is the head, even Christ (Ephesians 4:14-15).

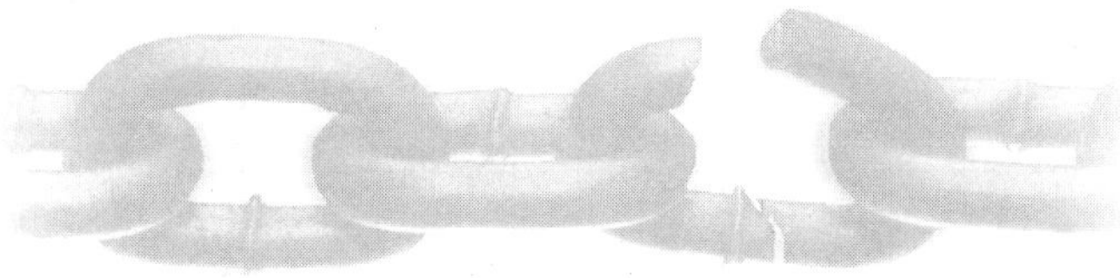

Learning from the Teacher provides the solid basis that keeps you from being tossed from one false doctrine to the next fad religion.

Stand firmly on His Truth.

DAY 12

Teacher's Pet

Ask of Me, and I will give You the nations for Your inheritance, and the ends of the earth for Your possession (Psalm 2:8 NKJV).

REFLECTION

There's no way that you can be the kind of student who goes into overtime and not become the teacher's pet. Remember seeing them in school—those students who always were in the teacher's face, and the teacher just loved them? They always asked why, as if everything the teacher discussed was so interesting. You were probably like me, always so bored and so sick of them, you wanted to hit them in the head with an apple. They just kept asking why, and the teacher seemed to enjoy them so much. They had established that teacher-to-student, student-to-teacher relationship. God says, "Don't sit in My class and be reluctant to ask questions. I'm the Master Teacher, the Good Master Teacher." God says, "If you really want to know, ask Me, and I will give you the heathen for an inheritance..." (see Ps. 2:8). If you really want to get something going with Me, start draining from the milk of My wisdom, start pulling from Me.

(POWER FOR LIVING, Chapter 4)

POWER LIVING PERSPECTIVE

1. Were you annoyed by the teacher's pet in school? What made that student different from you and the other students? Did you ever wish you could be like that student?

2. Were you ever the teacher's pet in school? How did that make you feel? How can you become *the* Teacher's pet?

3. "God wants us to question Him that we may find clarity and find effective solutions to the problems confronting us day in and day out." What does it mean to your life if you seek *His* wisdom to solve your problems and answer your questions?

4. "God says, 'Don't sit in My class and be reluctant to ask questions. I'm the Master Teacher, the Good Master Teacher.'" What keeps you from asking the hard questions?

5. The more time you spend in the Teacher's presence, the more wisdom you gain—the more you become like Him. In what ways do you think you will change after you have earned your first degree from the school of the Spirit?

MEDITATION

Ask, and it shall be given you; seek, and ye shall find; knock, and it shall be opened unto you (Matthew 7:7).

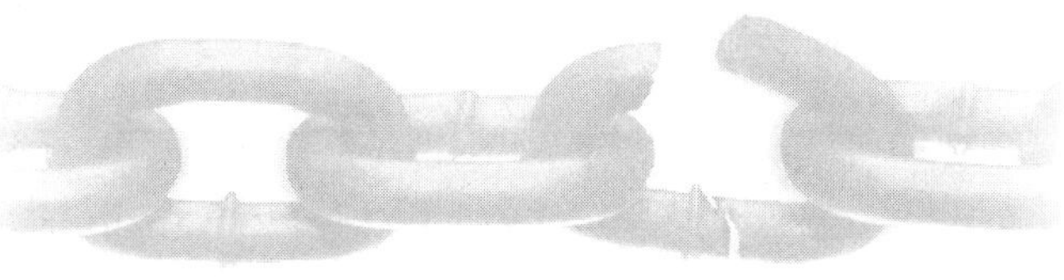

Ask—seek—knock!

DAY 13

PETER, THE MASTER TEACHER'S PET

Then Peter answered and said to Him, "Explain this parable to us" (Matthew 15:15 NKJV).

REFLECTION

The Church exists today as a result of the obedience and faithfulness of the twelve disciples, minus one (Judas). So it is quite evident that Jesus was an enormously good, proficient, and effective Teacher for eleven of His twelve men to go on and change the entire world and course of all humankind. No other teacher, school, or university can claim such success and effectiveness.

However, out of the twelve men, one stood out above all the rest. It was Peter. He later became known as the apostle Peter, the one Jesus called a *rock*. A very unique and passionate quality about this disciple distinguished him from the other eleven. That quality was Peter's dogged determination to understand issues. He was known for always asking why.

No doubt the other disciples thought Peter was a bigmouth. They probably said he talked too much. They probably felt that Peter thought he was a know-it-all, but it was Peter's tendency to always ask why that caused Jesus, the Teacher, to notice this loudmouthed man and reward him with the much-desired position of Teacher's pet. Notice, I said *reward* and not *appoint*.

(POWER FOR LIVING, Chapter 4)

Power Living Perspective

1. "You may be appointed to be a disciple but you have to earn the right—through diligence to know truth—to be the Teacher's pet." Realizing that you have the power through His anointing to be His most-favored child, what steps will you take to be the Teacher's pet?

2. "Jesus knew that if enough of Peter's whys were answered, then the loudmouthed, nosy, obnoxious fisherman would eventually become a great leader and apostle that God could use to get the world's attention." Do you fear others thinking of you as obnoxious? Does that keep you from becoming the Teacher's pet? How can you overcome that feeling?

3. It is evident that Jesus gave more attention to the development of three of the disciples—Peter, James, and John—than the other nine. Search for Scriptures that confirm this statement. Write them down and consider why these three were favored.

4. "Through Peter's persistence in asking questions, he initiated an exchange that developed a relationship between student and teacher. Every time something sacred and significant happened in Jesus' life and ministry, Peter was there." When God makes something significant happen today, do you want to be part of it?

5. "If we are willing to ask God why and let Him transform us into receiving His will, God will show us His favor and answer the whys of our heart." Do you believe this?

MEDITATION

Now after six days Jesus took Peter, James, and John, and led them up on a high mountain apart by themselves; and He was transfigured before them (Mark 9:2 NKJV).

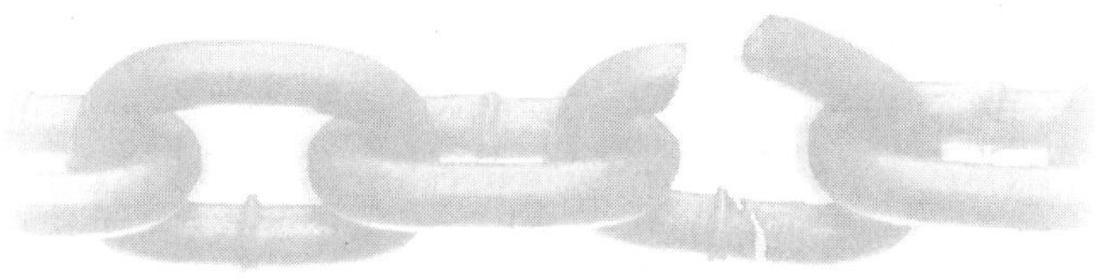

Dream about being one of the three with Jesus that day.

DAY

14

POWER AND COMPASSION

And they brought young children to Him, that He should touch them: and His disciples rebuked those that brought them. But when Jesus saw it, He was much displeased, and said unto them, "Suffer the little children to come unto Me, and forbid them not: for of such is the kingdom of God. Verily I say unto you, Whosoever shall not receive the kingdom of God as a little child, he shall not enter therein." And He took them up in His arms, put His hands upon them, and blessed them (Mark 10:13-16).

REFLECTION

It is interesting to me that just before the incident in Mark 10 took place, the Lord was ministering on the subject of divorce and adultery. When He brought up that subject, someone brought the children to Him so He could touch them.

Who were these nameless persons who had the insight and the wisdom to bring the children to the Master? (See Mark 10:13-16.) They brought the children to Him that He might touch them. What a strange interruption to a discourse on adultery and divorce. Here are these little children dragging dirty blankets and blank gazes into the presence of a God who is dealing with grown-up problems. He takes time from His busy schedule not so much to counsel them, but just to touch them. That's all it takes. *There is power in compassion.*

I salute all the wonderful people who work with children. Whether through children's church or public school, you have a very high calling. Don't forget to touch their little lives with a word of hope and a smile of encouragement. It may be the only one some will receive. You are the builders of our future. Be careful, for you may be building a house that we will have to live in!

(POWER FOR LIVING, Chapter 5)

POWER LIVING PERSPECTIVE

1. What does Jesus' reaction to the children say about His attitude toward the innocent? How can you convey compassion to the innocents around you?

2. Many children today are from broken homes. How can the healing touch of Jesus bring hope into their lives? Are there ways you can help children in your family, church, neighborhood? List several steps you can take to bring healing to a child.

3. If you are not called to be a teacher or a caregiver for children, what are other ways to share God's love with them?

4. "Don't forget to touch their little lives with a word of hope and a smile of encouragement. It may be the only one some will receive." Seeing children in distress can be hard on people. How can you overcome the feeling that prevents you from reaching out?

5. Pray that all those who care for and teach children—teachers, pastors, nurses, doctors, daycare workers—will give them hope, encouragement, and love. Write your prayer, and return to it often.

MEDITATION

Then they brought little children to Him, that He might touch them; but the disciples rebuked those who brought them. But when Jesus saw it, He was greatly displeased and said to them, "Let the little children come to Me, and do not forbid them; for of such is the kingdom of God. Assuredly, I say to you, whoever does not receive the kingdom of God as a little child will by no means enter it." And He took them up in His arms, laid His hands on them, and blessed them (Mark 10:13-16 NKJV).

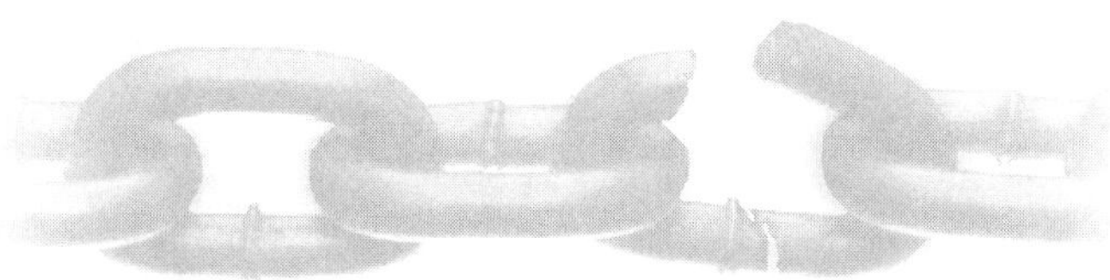

Children are our future.
Embrace them—and it—today.

DAY 15

SUFFER THE SUFFERING

But we see Jesus, who was made a little lower than the angels, for the suffering of death crowned with glory and honor, that He, by the grace of God, might taste death for everyone (Hebrews 2:9 NKJV).

REFLECTION

What was wrong with the disciples that they became angry at some nameless persons who aimed these little arrows toward the only Answer they might ever have gotten to see? Who told the disciples they were too busy to heal their own children? Jesus stopped teaching on the cause of divorce and marital abuse to touch the victim, to minister to the effect of the abuse. He told them to suffer the little children to come. Suffer the suffering to come! It is hard to work with hurting people, but the time has come for us to suffer the suffering to come. Anything that is hurt, whether an injured animal or a hospital patient, is unhappy.

We cannot get a wounded lion to jump through hoops! Hurting children as well as hurting adults can carry the unpleasant aroma of bitterness. In spite of the challenge, it is foolish to give up on your own. So they brought the "ouch" to the Band-Aid, and He stopped His message for His mission. Imagine tiny hands outstretched, little faces upturned, perching like sparrows on His knee. They came to get a touch, but He always gives us more than we expect. He held them with His loving arms. He touched with His sensitive hands. But most of all, He blessed them with His compassionate heart!

(POWER FOR LIVING, Chapter 5)

Power Living Perspective

1. Think about the people you work with, the people in your neighborhood, those in the pew beside you. Are some suffering? How can you share your power for living with them?

2. "It is hard to work with hurting people, but the time has come for us to suffer the suffering to come." What is the worst part of reaching out to someone who is hurting? What steps can you take to overcome that part?

3. "He stopped His message for His mission." Jesus was teaching a message when the children were brought to Him. He stopped and blessed them. He knows when we need a word or a touch. Keep your heart and spirit open to receive both.

4. "How can we be in the presence of a loving God and then not love little ones? When Jesus blessed the children, He challenged the adults to become as children." List five ways you can become childlike in the presence of a loving God.

5. Allowing God to hold you in His arms gives you the power to be compassionate. Who needs to feel your loving arms around them? Who needs a hug to forge ahead?

MEDITATION

And when she opened it, she saw the child, and behold, the baby wept. So she had compassion on him, and said, "This is one of the Hebrews' children" (Exodus 2:6 NKJV).

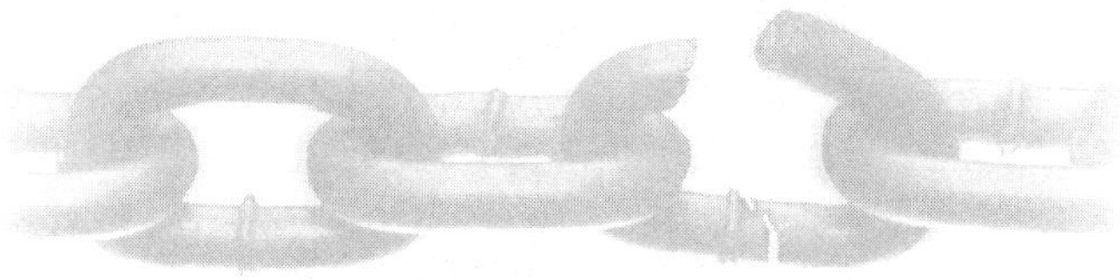

Because Pharaoh's daughter had compassion for the child Moses, a nation was saved.

What "nations" are depending on you for a compassionate response?

DAY 16

STARTING OVER

Then I passed by and saw you kicking about in your blood, and as you lay there in your blood I said to you, "Live!" I made you grow like a plant of the field. You grew up and developed and became the most beautiful of jewels. Your breasts were formed and your hair grew, you who were naked and bare. Later I passed by, and when I looked at you and saw that you were old enough for love, I spread the corner of My garment over you and covered your nakedness. I gave you My solemn oath and entered into a covenant with you, declares the Sovereign Lord, and you became Mine. I bathed you with water and washed the blood from you and put ointments on you. I clothed you with an embroidered dress and put leather sandals on you. I dressed you in fine linen and covered you with costly garments (Ezekiel 16:6-10 NIV).

REFLECTION

In God, we can become children again. Salvation is God giving us a chance to start over again. He will not abuse the children that come to Him. Through praise, I approach Him like a toddler on unskillful legs. In worship, I kiss His face and am held by the caress of His anointing. He has no ulterior motive, for His caress is safe and wholesome. It is so important that we learn how to worship and adore Him, for in both is power for living. There is no better way to climb into His arms. Even if you were exposed to grown-up situations when you were a child, God can reverse what you've been through. He'll let the grown-up person experience the joy of being a child in the presence of God!

Reach out and embrace the fact that God has been watching over you all your life. He covers you, He clothes you, and He blesses you! Rejoice in Him in spite of the broken places. God's grace is sufficient for your needs and your scars. He will anoint you with oil. The anointing of the Lord be upon you now! May it bathe, heal, and strengthen you as never before.

(POWER FOR LIVING, Chapter 5)

Power Living Perspective

1. "Salvation is God giving us a chance to start over again." Are you grateful for a chance to start over? What circumstance first comes to mind that you are glad to leave behind? Do you believe that God has taken care of that situation?

2. "Rejoice in Him in spite of the broken places. God's grace is sufficient for your needs and your scars." Every person suffers from time to time—how can you call on His power for living to get you past the scars?

3. Is Christ locked up behind your fears, your problems, your past, or your insecurities? What steps must you take to release His glory in your life? Determine today to take one of those steps.

4. God's anointing will bathe, heal, and strengthen you. Explain how you believe this happens.

5. "Reach out and embrace the fact that God has been watching over you all your life. He covers you, He clothes you, and He blesses you!" List ten things He has done for you recently. Make it a habit to thank Him for ten things He has done for you each day.

Meditation

Then He who sat on the throne said, "Behold, I make all things new." And He said to me, "Write, for these words are true and faithful" (Revelation 21:5 NKJV).

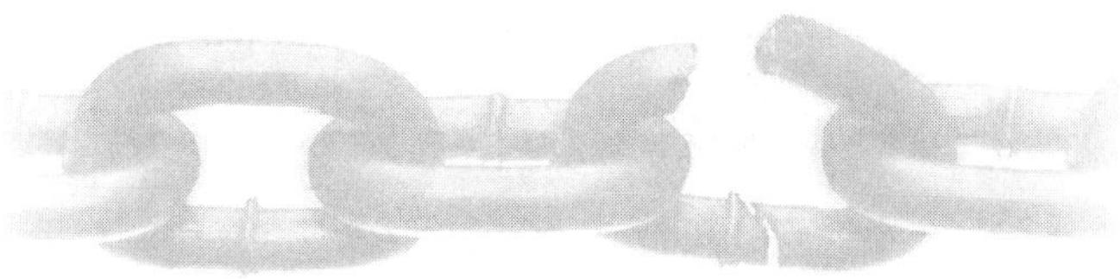

The anointing of God restores us and allows us to accomplish great and noble things. Believe it!

DAY
17

ATTITUDE

And Mary said, "Behold the handmaid of the Lord; be it unto me according to Thy word." And the angel departed from her (Luke 1:38).

REFLECTION

"Be it unto me according to Thy word." Not according to my marital status. Not according to my job. Not according to what I deserve. "Be it unto me according to Thy word."

Attitudes affect the way we live our lives. A good attitude can bring success. A poor attitude can bring destruction. An attitude results from perspective. I'm sure you understand what perspective is. Everyone seems to have a different perspective. It comes from the way we look at life, and the way we look at life is often determined by our history.

The events of the past can cause us to have an outlook or perspective on life that is less than God's perspective. The little girl who was abused learns to defend herself by not trusting men. This attitude of defensiveness often stretches into adulthood. If we have protected ourselves a certain way in the past with some measure of success, then it is natural to continue that pattern throughout life. Unfortunately, we often need to learn how to look past our perspective and change our attitudes.

(POWER FOR LIVING, Chapter 5)

POWER LIVING PERSPECTIVE

1. How would you rate your general attitude? 10=very positive; 1=very negative; or somewhere in between? Would your family agree with that rating? Why or why not?

2. "The events of the past can cause us to have an outlook or perspective on life that is less than God's perspective." Do you agree that your past reflects your perspective, which determines your attitude about many circumstances?

3. Is there something in your past or your current situation that has changed your attitude for the worst? For the best? Write about them. Focus more on what changed your attitude for the best.

____

____

____

____

____

____

____

4. "If we have protected ourselves a certain way in the past with some measure of success, then it is natural to continue that pattern throughout life." Explain a protective measure you have in place—and how you can instead trust God to release you from the hurt that caused you to build that defense.

____

____

____

____

____

____

5. List a few ways you can look past your perspective and change your attitude for the better.

Meditation

For My thoughts are not your thoughts, nor are your ways My ways," says the Lord. "For as the heavens are higher than the earth, so are My ways higher than your ways, and My thoughts than your thoughts (Isaiah 55:8-9 NKJV).

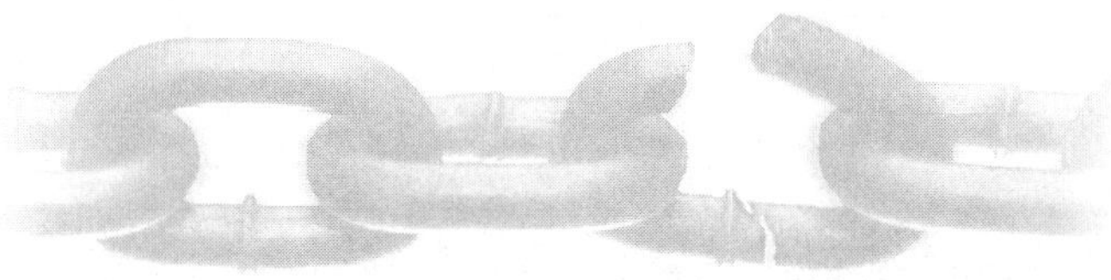

God takes the unlikely and infuses them with His power, revelation, and wisdom so they can be wondrously educated in the things of God. This occurs so they can greatly change and affect the things of the world. Are you ready?

DAY

18

Victorious Power

Then Amnon hated her exceedingly, so that the hatred with which he hated her was greater than the love with which he had loved her. And Amnon said to her, "Arise, be gone!" So she said to him, "No, indeed! This evil of sending me away is worse than the other that you did to me." But he would not listen to her (2 Samuel 13:15-16 NKJV).

REFLECTION

Have you ever had anything happen to you that changed you forever? Somehow you were like a palm tree that bends with the wind and you survived. Yet you knew you would never be the same. Perhaps you have spent every day since then bowed over. You could in no way lift up yourself. You shout. You sing. You skip. But when no one is looking, when the crowd is gone and the lights are out, you are still that trembling, crying, bleeding mass of pain that is abused, bowed, bent backward, and crippled.

Maybe you have gone through divorces, tragedies, and adulterous relationships, and you've been left feeling unwanted. You can't shout over that sort of thing. You can't leap over that kind of wall. It injures something about you that changes how you relate to everyone else for the rest of your life.

Amnon didn't even want Tamar afterward. She pleaded with him, "Don't throw me away." She was fighting for the last strands of her femininity. Amnon called a servant and said, "Throw her out."

(POWER FOR LIVING, Chapter 6)

Power Living Perspective

1. What do you do when you are trapped in a transitory state, neither in nor out? You're left lying at the door, torn up and disturbed, trembling and intimidated.

2. You may have been physically or emotionally raped and robbed. You survived, but you left a substantial degree of self-esteem in Amnon's bed. Have you lost the road map that directs you back to where you were before? Do you know someone who needs direction back to before?

3. "The Lord says, 'I want you. I will give you power for living. No matter how many Amnons have said they don't want you—I want you.'" Emotional and physical abuse is hard to get through. Only God can totally and completely wash away the pain. Have you forgiven those in your past who have caused you harm? Write their names and after each, write why you have (or have not) forgiven them.

4. In Luke 13:10-17 Jesus called forth the wounded, hurting woman. He restored her completely. Do you believe that Jesus can see beyond wounds and hurts to heal your every infirmity? Read the passage in Luke and then describe the scene in your own words.

5. God sees your struggles and He knows about your pain. He knows what happened to you ten years ago, ten months ago, and even last week. What struggle is holding you back from accepting all of His grace and mercy?

Meditation

O Lord, You have searched me and You know me. You know when I sit and when I rise; You perceive my thoughts from afar. You discern my going out and my lying down; You are familiar with all my ways. Before a word is on my tongue You know it completely, O Lord (Psalm 139:1-4 NIV).

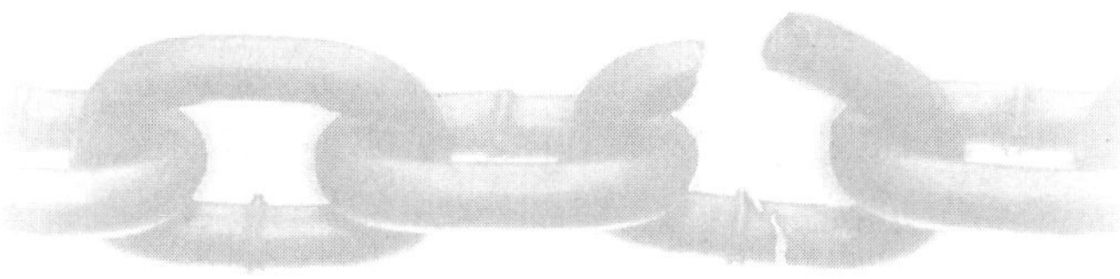

Don't be embarrassed or intimidated by the fact that God knows you inside out.

Rejoice that He knows you so well—and loves you anyway!

DAY
19

BY MY SPIRIT

...Not by might, nor by power, but by My spirit, saith the Lord of hosts (Zechariah 4:6).

REFLECTION

The anointing power of the living God is reaching out to you. He calls you forth to set you free. When you reach out to Him and allow the Holy Spirit to have His way, His anointing is present to deliver you. Demons will tremble. Satan wants to keep you at the door but never let you enter. He wants to keep you down, but now his power is broken in your life.

Tamar knew the feeling of desertion. She understood that she was cast out. However, the Bible explains that Absalom came and said, "I'm going to take you in." You too may have been lying at the door. Perhaps you didn't have anywhere to go. You may have been half in and half out. You were broken and demented and disturbed. But God sent His Absalom to restore you.

(POWER FOR LIVING, Chapter 6)

Power Living Perspective

1. "In this instance, Absalom depicts the purpose of real ministry. Thank God for the Church. It's the place where you can come broken and disgusted, and be healed, delivered, and set free in the name of Jesus." Have you witnessed this type of Church experience?

2. Have you ever had a Church experience that was less than you expected? Write about it.

3. Have you had a Church experience that was much more than you expected? Write about it.

4. If you could create the perfect Church experience, what would it be like? Describe it in detail.

5. Does your church have a ministry focused on restoring emotionally or physically abused people? Why or why not?

MEDITATION

The Spirit of the Lord is upon Me, because He hath anointed Me to preach the gospel to the poor; He hath sent Me to heal the brokenhearted, to preach deliverance to the captives, and recovering of sight to the blind, to set at liberty them that are bruised (Luke 4:18).

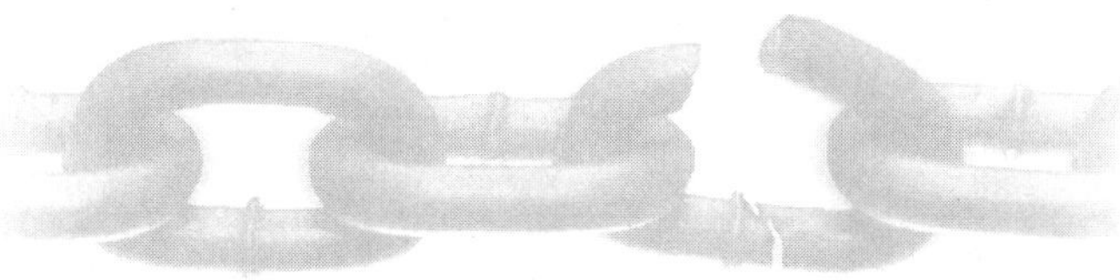

Are you moved by the Spirit of the Lord to reach out to the poor, brokenhearted, captive, blind, and bruised?

Pray for a heart that is open to help others.

DAY
20

FREEDOM NOW!

Come now, and let us reason together, saith the Lord: though your sins be as scarlet, they shall be as white as snow; though they be red like crimson, they shall be as wool (Isaiah 1:18).

REFLECTION

You may have thought that you would never rejoice again. God declares that you can have freedom in Him—now! The joy that He brings can be restored to your soul. He identifies with your pain and suffering. He knows what it is like to suffer abuse at the hands of others. Yet He proclaims joy and strength. He will give you the garment of praise instead of the spirit of heaviness (see Isa. 61:3).

Once you have called out to Him, you can lift up your hands in praise. No matter what you have suffered, you can hold up your head. Regardless of who has hurt you, hold up your head!

Like Tamar, you're a survivor. You should celebrate your survival. Instead of agonizing over your tragedies, you should celebrate your victory and thank God you made it. I charge you to step over your adversity and walk into the newness. It is like stepping from a storm into the sunshine—step into it now.

(POWER FOR LIVING, Chapter 6)

Power Living Perspective

1. "When you have suffered, it makes you able to relate to other people's pain." Knowing "how they feel" gives you power to comfort...and be comforted. Have you helped someone through the same tough time you had experienced previously?

2. Jesus identifies with your pain and suffering because He knows what it's like to suffer abuse at the hands of others. When considering what Jesus went through, how does your situation compare with His? Write about it.

3. After you have called out to Him, you can lift up your hands in praise. Lifting holy hands releases the pain and welcomes the power for living. Lift your hands and praise Him for the next few moments—welcome His presence.

4. "And the Lord restored Job's losses when he prayed for his friends. Indeed the Lord gave Job twice as much as he had before" (Job 42:10 NKJV). Not only will God give you victory and freedom from your past hurts, He will give you even more than you expected. Do you believe this? Why or why not?

5. "Even now, after all you've been through, God has the power to raise you up again! This is the *present* tense of faith. Walk into your newness even now." Write about how you have been anointed with victorious power.

Meditation

And the Lord restored Job's losses when he prayed for his friends. Indeed the Lord gave Job twice as much as he had before (Job 42:10 NKJV).

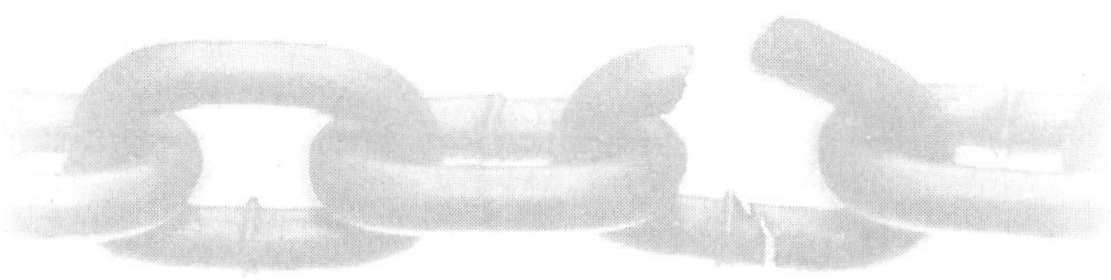

**Job suffered much, but his family and possessions were restored.
Are you ready to receive twice as much?**

DAY

21

POWER OVER FEAR

But seek the kingdom of God, and all these things shall be added to you. "Do not fear, little flock, for it is your Father's good pleasure to give you the kingdom (Luke 12:31-32 NKJV).

REFLECTION

Fear is as lethal to us as paralysis of the brain. It makes our thoughts become arthritic and our memory sluggish. It is the kind of feeling that can make a graceful person stumble up the stairs in a crowd. You know what I mean—the thing that makes the articulate stutter and the rhythmic become spastic. Like an oversized growth, fear soon becomes impossible to camouflage. Telltale signs like trembling knees or quivering lips betray fear even in the most disciplined person. Fear is the nightmare of the stage; it haunts the hearts of the timid as well as of the intimidated.

Remembering a time when fear gripped me, even now I can only speculate how long it took for the fear to give way to normalcy, or for the distant rumble of my racing heart to recede into the steadiness of practical thinking and rationality. I can't estimate time because fear traps time and holds it hostage in a prison of icy anxiety. Eventually, though, like the thawing of icicles on the roof of an aged and sagging house, my heart gradually melted into a steady and less pronounced beat.

(POWER FOR LIVING, Chapter 7)

POWER LIVING PERSPECTIVE

1. Fear paralyzes the brain and causes negativity. Explain the opposite of fear and how it positively contributes to a healthy state of mind.

2. What was your greatest fear as a child? Have you completely overcome that fear? Why or why not?

3. What is your current greatest fear? Can you give it over to God for disposal? If not, why not?

4. If you truly believe that "greater is He who is in you than he who is in the world" (see 1 John 4:4), what part can fear play in your life?

5. What is the difference between fear and worry? Does God allow either? (See Matthew 6:25-34.)

MEDITATION

*And the angel said unto them, "**Fear not**: for, behold, I bring you good tidings of great joy, which shall be to all people"* (Luke 2:10).

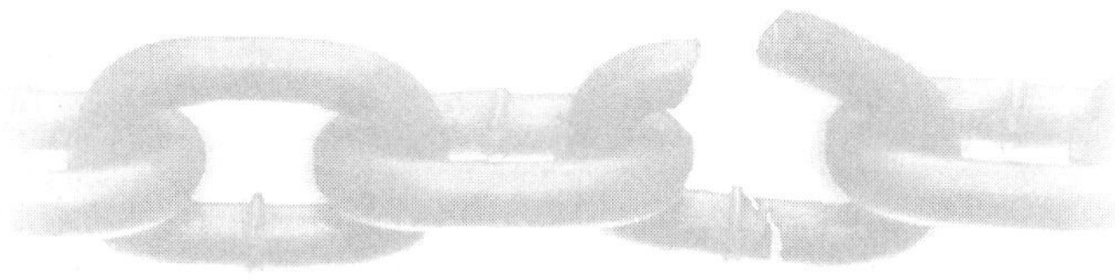

Listen for the angels telling you to "fear not," and take their advice seriously.

DAY
22

FATHERHOOD

For ye have ***not*** *received the spirit of bondage again to fear; but ye have received the Spirit of adoption, whereby we cry, Abba, Father* (Romans 8:15).

REFLECTION

When the disciples asked Jesus to teach them to pray, the first thing He taught them was to acknowledge the *fatherhood* of God. When we say "Our Father," we acknowledge His fatherhood and declare our relationship as it relates to the privilege of belonging to His divine family. Similarly, one of the first words most babies say is "Daddy." So knowing your father helps you understand your own identity as a son or daughter. Greater still is the need to know not only *who* your father is, but *how he feels about you.*

It is not good to deny a child the right to feel his father's love. In divorce cases, some women use the children to punish their ex-husbands. Because of her broken covenant with the child's father, the mother may deny him the right to see his child. This is not good for the child! Every child is curious about his father.

(POWER FOR LIVING, Chapter 7)

Power Living Perspective

1. "Every child is curious about his father." How curious are you about your heavenly Father? Curious enough to study His love letter to you? Read Psalm 46 and write about your Father's faithfulness in times of trouble.

2. "Greater still is the need to know not only *who* your father is, but *how he feels about you*." If you had a less-than-attentive earthly father, realize that your heavenly Father is always willing to listen, come alongside, and reassure you. Describe your vision of a perfect earthly father—then know that God the Father is above and beyond your imagination.

3. If you are a father, do your children know how you feel about them? Why or why not?

4. What can you do to assure your children that you love them and want them to grow strong in the knowledge of the Lord?

5. If you are holding unforgiveness against your earthly father, decide today to soften your heart toward him. Ask your heavenly Father to give you the power to forgive and make amends.

MEDITATION

Forgive us our sins, for we also forgive everyone who sins against us. And lead us not into temptation (Luke 11:4 NIV).

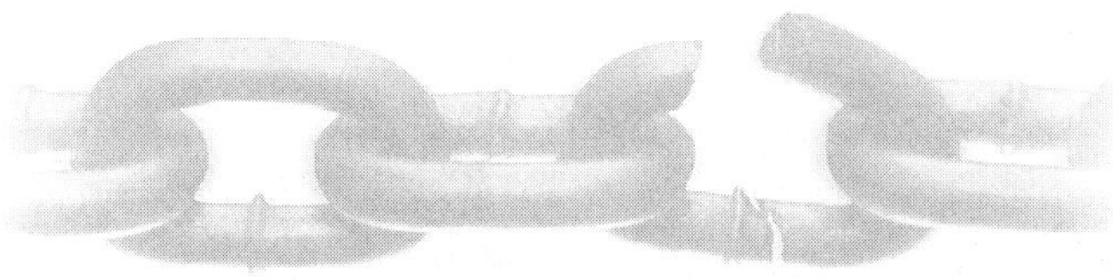

Heavenly Father, thank You for welcoming and loving me into Your family!

DAY
23
WHAT A RELIEF

What a fellowship, what a joy divine,
Leaning on the everlasting arms;
What a blessedness, what a peace is mine,
Leaning on the everlasting arms.
Leaning, leaning, safe and secure from all alarms;
Leaning, leaning, leaning on the everlasting arms.

Oh, how sweet to walk in this pilgrim way,
Leaning on the everlasting arms;
Oh, how bright the path grows from day to day,
Leaning on the everlasting arms.

Leaning, leaning, safe and secure from all alarms;
Leaning, leaning, leaning on the everlasting arms.
What have I to dread, what have I to fear,

Leaning on the everlasting arms?
I have blessed peace with my Lord so near,
Leaning on the everlasting arms.

Leaning, leaning, safe and secure from all alarms;
Leaning, leaning, leaning on the everlasting arms.[1]

ENDNOTE

1 Elisha A. Hoffman, *Leaning On the Everlasting Arms*, 1887.

REFLECTION

What a relief to learn that God can carry the load even better than my natural father could and that He will never leave me nor forsake me! Perhaps it was this holy refuge that inspired the hymnist to pen the words, "What a fellowship, what a joy divine, leaning on the everlasting arms."

I have been in the delivery room with my wife as she was giving birth. I witnessed the pain and suffering she endured. I believe that there were times of such intense pain that she would have shot me if she had been given a chance. Her desire made her continue. She didn't simply give up. She endured the pain so new life could be born. Once the child was born, the pain was soon forgotten.

Until the desire to go forward becomes greater than the memories of past pain, you will never hold the power to create again. However, when the desire comes back into your spirit and begins to live in you again, it will release you from the pain.

(POWER FOR LIVING, Chapter 7)

POWER LIVING PERSPECTIVE

1. Your desire to move forward will release you from the pain. Do you desire to more forward, or is it more comfortable to stay where you are?

2. Until you have a vision to go ahead, you will always live in yesterday's struggles. Solomon wrote, "Where there is no vision, the people perish" (Prov. 29:18a). Do you feel as if you are perishing? What can you do to get past your yesterdays?

3. The devil wants you to live in yesterday. He's always telling you about what you cannot do. His method is to bring up your past. What is the best way to deal with the devil according to God's Word? (See James 4:7.)

4. God is powerful enough to destroy the yoke of the enemy in your life. He is strong enough to bring you out and loose you, deliver you, and set you free. Search the Bible for Scriptures to support this promise. Write them in your own words.

5. Can you remember a time when you needed a hug? What happened? God's arms are always open—allow Him to wrap His loving arms around you. There is power for living in His embrace.

MEDITATION

I am still confident of this: I will see the goodness of the Lord in the land of the living (Psalm 27:13 NIV).

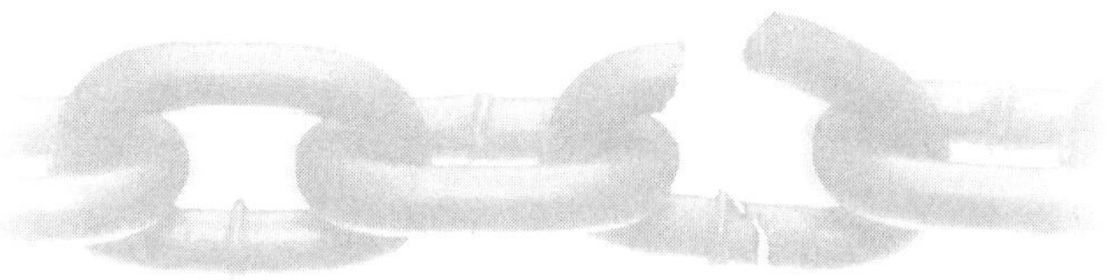

Expect something wonderful to happen!

DAY 24

POWER TO BELIEVE

I will praise Thee; for I am fearfully and wonderfully made: marvellous are Thy works; and that my soul knoweth right well (Psalm 139:14).

REFLECTION

The Book of Hebrews provides us with a tremendous lesson on faith. When we believe God, we are counted as righteous. Righteousness cannot be earned or merited. It comes only through faith. We can have a good report simply on the basis of our faith. Faith becomes the tender, like money is the legal tender that we use for exchange of goods and services in this world. Faith becomes the tender, or the substance, of things hoped for, and the evidence of things not seen. By it the elders obtained a good report (see Heb. 11:1-3).

The invisible became visible and was manifested. God wants us to understand that just because we can't see it doesn't mean that He won't do it. What God wants to do in us begins as a word that gets in our spirit. Everything that is tangible started as an intangible. It was a dream, a thought, a word of God. In the same way, what humankind has invented began as a concept in someone's mind. So just because we don't see it, doesn't mean we won't get it.

(POWER FOR LIVING, Chapter 8)

POWER LIVING PERSPECTIVE

1. After reading Hebrews chapter 11, write what and who defines faith.

2. In your opinion, who is the most powerful faith reference in Hebrews chapter 11? Why?

3. In your opinion, what is the most exciting story about faith in Hebrews chapter 11? Why?

4. "These were all commended for their faith, yet none of them received what had been promised. God had planned something better for us so that only together with us would they be made perfect" (Heb. 11:39-40 NIV). What do these verses mean to you as a believer in the 21st century?

5. "God wants us to understand that just because we can't see it doesn't mean that He won't do it." What are you believing God for that you haven't *seen* yet?

MEDITATION

Now faith is the substance of things hoped for, the evidence of things not seen (Hebrews 11:1).

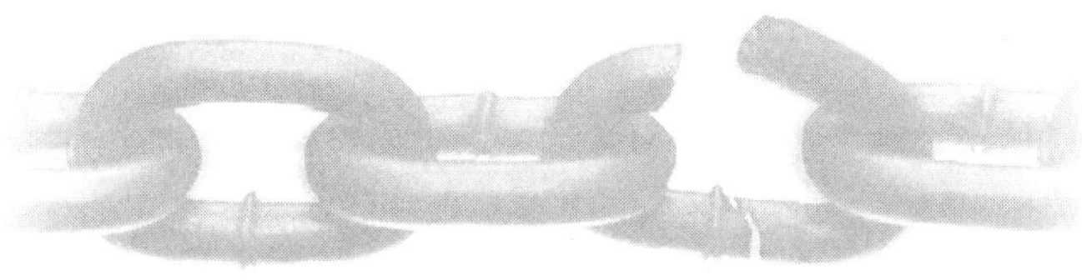

Great men and women of God have something in common—trust in the sovereignty of their almighty Lord.

DAY
25

SEEKING DILIGENT SEEKERS

But without faith it is impossible to please Him: for he that cometh to God must believe that He is, and that He is a rewarder of them that diligently seek Him (Hebrews 11:6).

REFLECTION

There is a progression in the characters mentioned in Hebrews chapter 11. Abel worshiped God by faith. Enoch walked with God by faith. You can't walk with God until you worship God. The first calling is to learn how to worship God. When you learn how to worship God, then you can develop a walk with Him. Stop trying to get people to walk with God who won't worship. If you don't love Him enough to worship, you'll never be able to walk with Him. If you can worship like Abel, then you can walk like Enoch.

Enoch walked, and by faith Noah worked with God. You can't work with God until you walk with God. You can't walk with God until you worship God. If you can worship like Abel, then you can walk like Enoch. And if you walk like Enoch, then you can work like Noah.

(POWER FOR LIVING, Chapter 8)

Power Living Perspective

1. Who do you most identify with?

   ___Worship like Abel

   ___Walk like Enoch

   ___Work like Noah

   Explain your reasoning.

2. "God will reward those who persevere in seeking Him. He may not come when you want Him to, but He will be right on time." Believing that He will be "right on time" relieves you of having to watch the clock of life. Thank Him for something that did indeed happen at the right time.

3. "God's power will loose the bands from around your neck." Do you sometimes feel as if there is a choke hold keeping you from reaching your potential? Accepting God's anointing will break that hold on your life. Write a prayer to accept His powerful anointing.

4. Abraham was mentioned several times in Hebrews chapter 11. What was Sarah applauded for? (See Hebrews 11:11.) Think of a time when you forged ahead on faith knowing that God would meet you in the end. Write about it.

5. Sarah had a baby after she was past childbearing age. Mary had a baby without "knowing" a man. List a few other miracles that God provided for those who had faith.

Meditation

Jesus answered and said unto them, Verily I say unto you, "If ye have faith, and doubt not, ye shall not only do this which is done to the fig tree, but also if ye shall say unto this mountain, 'Be thou removed, and be thou cast into the sea'; it shall be done" (Matthew 21:21).

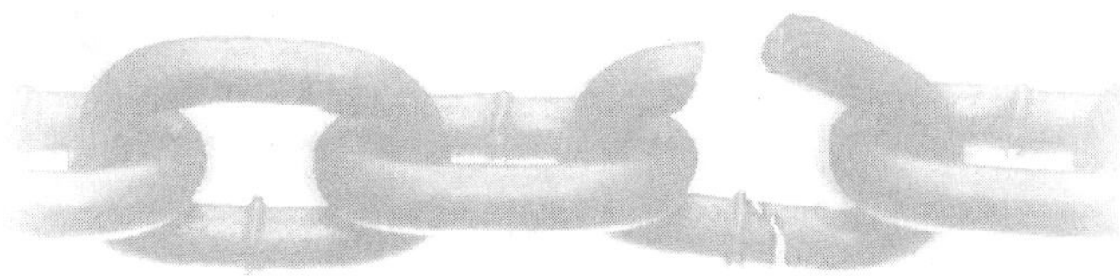

Do you have mountain-moving faith?

DAY
26

FEAR OR RESPECT?

And unto man He said, Behold, the fear of the Lord, that is wisdom; and to depart from evil is understanding (Job 28:28).

REFLECTION

The Hebrew term for "fear" in this verse is *yir'ah*, according to *Strong's Exhaustive Concordance of the Bible*. It means a moral fear, or reverence. So what attitude should we have toward our heavenly Father? The Bible declares that we should have a strong degree of reverence for Him. But a distinction must be made here: there is a great deal of difference between fear and reverence.

The term *reverence* means to respect or revere; but the term *fear* carries with it a certain connotation of terror and intimidation. That kind of fear is not a healthy attitude for a child of God to have about his heavenly Father. The term rendered *fear* in Job 28:28 could be better translated as *respect*. Fear will drive man away from God like it drove Adam to hide in the bushes at the sound of the voice of his only Deliverer. Adam said, "I heard Thy voice in the garden, and I was afraid…" (Gen. 3:10). That is not the reaction a loving father wants from his children. I don't want my children to scatter and hide like mice when I approach! I may not always agree with what they have done, but I will always love who they are.

(POWER FOR LIVING, Chapter 8)

POWER LIVING PERSPECTIVE

1. Are you afraid of God? Why or why not?

2. Do you respect God? In what ways do you respect Him? How do you show respect for Him?

3. Was Adam's fear justified? Why?

4. Are your children afraid of you, or do they respect you? Explain.

5. Do you need an attitude adjustment when it comes to respecting and/or fearing your heavenly Father?

MEDITATION

But the mercy and loving-kindness of the Lord are from everlasting to everlasting upon those who reverently and worshipfully fear Him, and His righteousness is to children's children (Psalm 103:17 AMP).

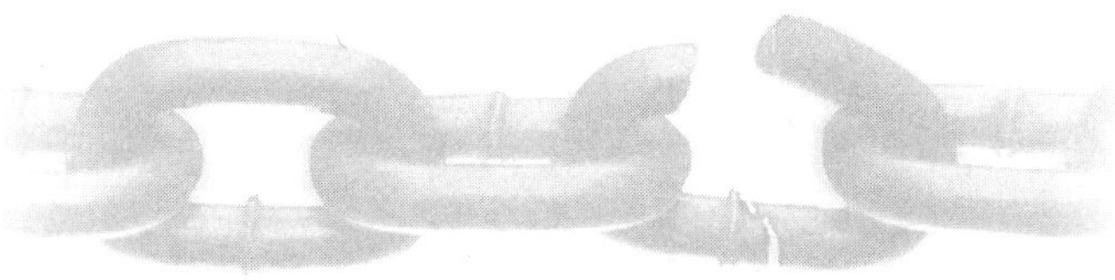

Oh friend, He may not approve of your conduct, but He still loves you! In fact, when you come to understand this fact, it will help you improve your conduct.

DAY

27

No Fear in Truth

"…true worshippers shall worship the Father in spirit and in truth: for the Father seeketh such [real people, flawed people like the woman at the well] to worship Him. God is a Spirit: and they that worship Him must worship Him in spirit and in truth" (John 4:23-24).

REFLECTION

We have nothing to fear, for our honesty with the Father doesn't reveal anything to Him that He doesn't already know! His intellect is so keen that He doesn't have to wait for you to make a mistake. He knows of your failure before you fail. His knowledge is all-inclusive, spanning the gaps between times and incidents. He knows our thoughts even as we unconsciously gather them together to make sense in our own mind!

Once we know this, all our attempts at silence and secrecy seem juvenile and ridiculous. He is "the all-seeing One," and He knows perfectly and completely what is in each of us. When we pray, and more importantly, when we commune with God, we must have the kind of confidence and assurance that neither requires nor allows deceit. Although my Father abhors my sin, He loves me. His love is incomprehensible, primarily because there is nothing with which we can compare it! What we must do is accept the riches of His grace and stand in the shade of His loving arms.

(POWER FOR LIVING, Chapter 8)

Power Living Perspective

1. "Trusting God with your successes isn't really a challenge. The real test of trust is to be able to share your secrets, your inner failures, and your fears." Think of your deepest, darkest secret. Now write about why you haven't given it over to God.

2. "What we must do is accept the riches of His grace and stand in the shade of His loving arms." Are you standing naked and ashamed—or are you standing in the cool shade of your Father's loving arms?

3. "A mutual enhancement comes into a relationship where there is intimacy based on honesty." Name a few people in the Bible who were less than truthful with God. What was their fate?

4. Honesty is the best policy when communicating with your heavenly Father. What secrets do you wish He didn't know about? Have you accepted the fact that He knows *all* your secrets and loves you in spite of them? Why or why not?

5. "The heroes in the Bible were not perfect, but they were powerful! They were not superhuman, but they were revelatory. Often chastised and corrected, they were still not discarded, for the Lord was with them." Name a few of God's "heroes" who were not "perfect." Also write *your* name!

MEDITATION

Brethren, I count not myself to have apprehended: but this one thing I do, forgetting those things which are behind, and reaching forth unto those things which are before, I press toward the mark for the prize of the high calling of God in Christ Jesus (Philippians 3:13-14).

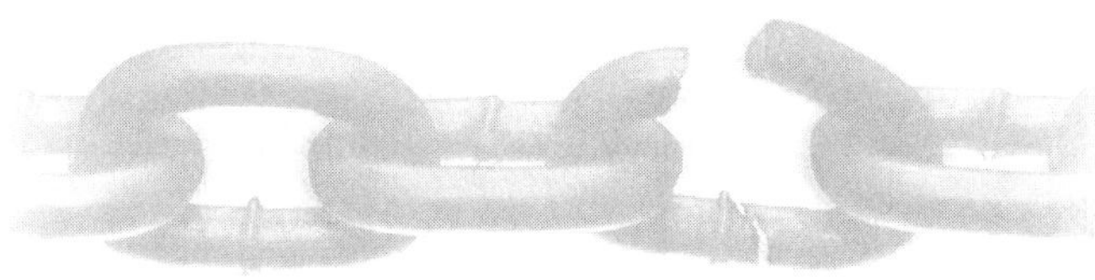

Press forward toward the prize!

DAY 28

ANOINTED POWER

Why do the heathen rage, and the people imagine a vain thing? The kings of the earth set themselves, and the rulers take counsel together, against the Lord, and against His anointed, saying, "Let us break Their bands asunder, and cast away Their cords from us." He that sitteth in the heavens shall laugh: the Lord shall have them in derision. Then shall He speak unto them in His wrath, and vex them in His sore displeasure. "Yet have I set My King upon My holy hill of Zion. I will declare the decree: the Lord hath said unto Me, 'Thou art My Son; this day have I begotten Thee. Ask of Me, and I shall give Thee the heathen for Thine inheritance, and the uttermost parts of the earth for Thy possession'" (Psalm 2:1-8).

REFLECTION

"Why do the heathen rage, and the people imagine a vain thing?" The actual question in this text is not King David asking God the motivation of those who take counsel (conspire) to come against the Lord and His anointed. More importantly, it is David asking God why He allows it to happen. "God, why do You allow the heathen to rage, and why do You let the rulers and kings of the earth set themselves against You and against Your anointed? Why God, *why?*"

Why does God allow His anointed to suffer so greatly? After all, the sole motivation of the anointed is to do the will of God. You would think that if the primary desire in the life of the anointed is to please their heavenly Father, the least He could do is protect and preserve them. You would think God would stop the persecution, mistreatment, and abuse by the heathens and phony church folks. But the truth of the matter is that God allows His anointed to go through—and in most cases sends them through—more than all others. An intelligent question is, "God, why?"

(POWER FOR LIVING, Chapter 9)

POWER LIVING PERSPECTIVE

1. Do you ever feel like David and ask God why certain things happen? Does He answer you? Do you expect an answer?

2. "God, why do You allow the heathen to rage, and why do You let the rulers and kings of the earth set themselves against You and against Your anointed?" Have there been times when the heathen raged around you? Describe the circumstance and situation. Were there those who stood for the Lord God?

3. Are there modern-day rulers and kings of the earth who have set themselves against God and His anointed? List them and their reasons.

4. "Why does God allow His anointed to suffer so greatly?" Give your answer.

5. "God allows His anointed to go through—and in most cases sends them through—more than all others." Why?

Meditation

Blessed are those who are persecuted because of righteousness, for theirs is the kingdom of heaven (Matthew 5:10 NIV).

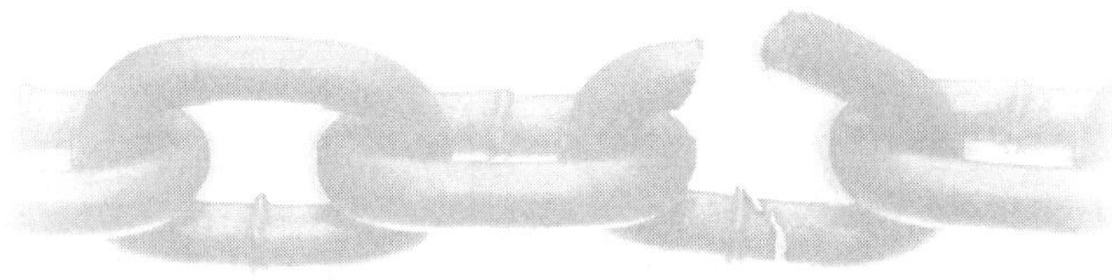

How blessed do you feel when you are being persecuted?

Do you believe yours is the Kingdom of Heaven?

DAY 29

JEALOUSY

And the great dragon was cast out, that old serpent, called the Devil, and Satan, which deceiveth the whole world: he was cast out into the earth, and his angels were cast out with him (Revelation 12:9).

REFLECTION

Jealousy is the manifestation of insecurity and dissatisfaction with one's calling and self-worth. When you don't know your purpose, you become discontent and many times become envious of another's success. Jealousy and bitter envying are the root cause of the spirit of competition. That spirit presently plagues many in church leadership and those aspiring to positions of leadership. Everybody wants to be number one, the top dog, the head honcho, the man or woman in demand.

So in our desire to be number one, we covet, lust, and compete for another's position, status, or possessions. Why do we do this? Because we want everybody to look at us, to like us, to admire us, to respect us, to worship us. Before we know it, we've become drunk with selfish ambition and, like satan, our hidden motives of the heart become the attitude of rebellion against who and what God has called us to be and do. If we don't come to our senses and repent, we will inevitably become deceived and overwhelmed with the lust for power, prestige, position, and possessions. We no longer aspire to love the Lord with all our heart, soul, strength, and mind.

(POWER FOR LIVING, Chapter 9)

Power Living Perspective

1. Are you jealous of someone? Write why.

2. What steps can you take to overcome your jealously?

3. When you have feelings of envy, lust, and jealousy, who is in control of your life?

4. When you have feelings of love, justice, and compassion, who is in control of your life?

5. What is the difference between selfish ambition and righteous motivation? Which most defines your attitude about succeeding in life?

MEDITATION

Anger is cruel and fury overwhelming, but who can stand before jealousy? (Proverbs 27:4 NIV)

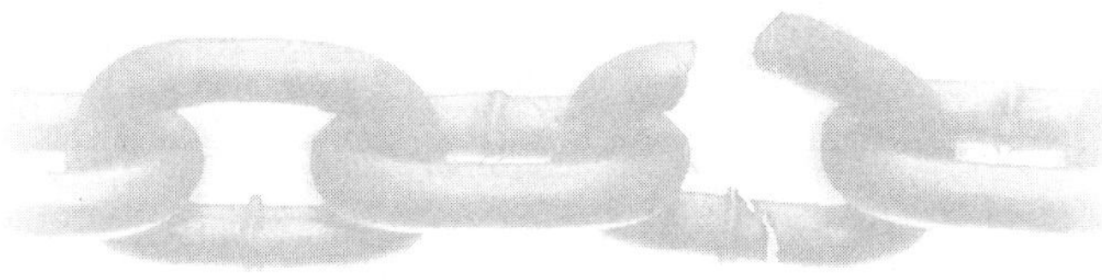

Jealousy is like a cancer that permeates your body with poison.

DAY 30

DEATH TO THE FLESH

This I say then, Walk in the Spirit, and ye shall not fulfil the lust of the flesh (Galatians 5:16).

REFLECTION

It is, without exception, absolutely necessary for the anointed to suffer. The moment you begin to accept and understand this, you will begin to rejoice in tribulation. I know this doesn't sit well with much of what we've been taught in reference to our victory in Christ. We do have victory in Christ, but we must understand that there has to be a battle fought in order to gain a victory. There is no victory without war. Also you have to know that just as God has promised to supply all our needs according to His riches in glory, He also has promised us trials and tribulations in this life. Tribulations and trials serve, by the aid of the Holy Spirit, a divine purpose. The purpose is death. Death? That's right, I mean death—death to the flesh.

If you are going to walk in the anointing, power, and presence of God, you must be dead to self. In order to be alive to Christ, you must first yield to the sanctifying work of the Holy Spirit and die to the works of the flesh. Why? *So that no flesh may glory in His sight* (see 1 Cor. 1:29). Before a man or woman is dead to self, they are occupied and consumed with self and how they can please themselves. They make a conscious decision to walk in their own understanding instead of acknowledging the Lord and being directed by His wisdom.

(POWER FOR LIVING, Chapter 9)

Power Living Perspective

1. Can there be victory in Christ without a war with the flesh? Why or why not?

2. Sometimes our self-made trials are harsher than life's tribulations. List a few problems you are facing that have been self-generated. How can you climb past these issues?

3. "If you are going to walk in the anointing, power, and presence of God, you must be dead to self." Write what "dead to self" means to you.

4. Can you ever be truly "dead to self"? Yes or No. Please explain.

5. Are you daily acknowledging the Lord and being directed by His wisdom?

MEDITATION

Which in time past were not a people, but are now the people of God: which had not obtained mercy, but now have obtained mercy. Dearly beloved, I beseech you as strangers and pilgrims, abstain from fleshly lusts, which war against the soul (1 Peter 2:10-11).

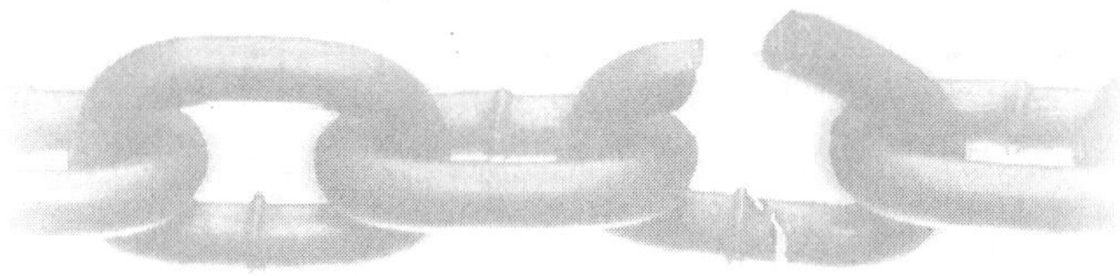

Today's society is rotting from pornography, sexual deviance, and disease.

Why is it so hard to deny the flesh?

DAY 31

A Hunk of Cheese

There hath no temptation taken you but such as is common to man: but God is faithful, who will not suffer you to be tempted above that ye are able; but will with the temptation also make a way to escape, that ye may be able to bear it (1 Corinthians 10:13).

REFLECTION

God is pleased and obsessed with being glorified and receiving glory from His creation. Many children of God have become overwhelmed with bewilderment and are confused as to why bad things always seem to happen to good people. But the answer is simple, my friend. God wants to be glorified. So every now and then you may find yourself tempted and pursued like a fugitive, wanted by the devil. The pressure, stress, and strain in your life may make you feel like a hunk of cheese on a mouse trap, ready to be eaten by the enemy. You may get the idea that God is using you like a pawn on a chess board, which is a game called *life* that you have no control over and cannot win.

The devil gets happy because he thinks you're down for the count. But God laughs! Why? Because God already knows that He will not allow you to go through anything, or be subjected to anything, beyond your anointing. God gives you ability to bear it. That's why He laughs and lets the devil sometimes have at you. God knows you're faithful. God knows that it's just a matter of time before satan pushes you so far that you will fall right back into the lap of goodness and mercy.

(POWER FOR LIVING, Chapter 9)

POWER LIVING PERSPECTIVE

1. "God is pleased and obsessed with being glorified and receiving glory from His creation." List five ways you can please God today. List five ways you can glorify Him *every* day.

2. Do you ever feel like a "hunk of cheese on a mouse trap, ready to be eaten by the enemy"? How can you quickly turn yourself into a mouth-watering delight for the Lord's glory rather than satan's lunch?

3. "You may get the idea that God is using you like a pawn on a chess board, which is a game called *life* that you have no control over and cannot win." Why do you feel this way sometimes? Or maybe you've never felt that God is a gamesman who is using you. If so, write why you disagree with this statement.

4. "The devil gets happy because he thinks you're down for the count." Write about a time when the devil was happy because of the situation you were going through. When you overcame the problem, could you feel the devil flee?

5. Every believer needs the power of God to get through each and every day. Are you feeling weak today? Pray for God's anointing power. Write what you hope His answer will be.

MEDITATION

There is therefore now no condemnation to them which are in Christ Jesus, who walk not after the flesh, but after the Spirit (Romans 8:1).

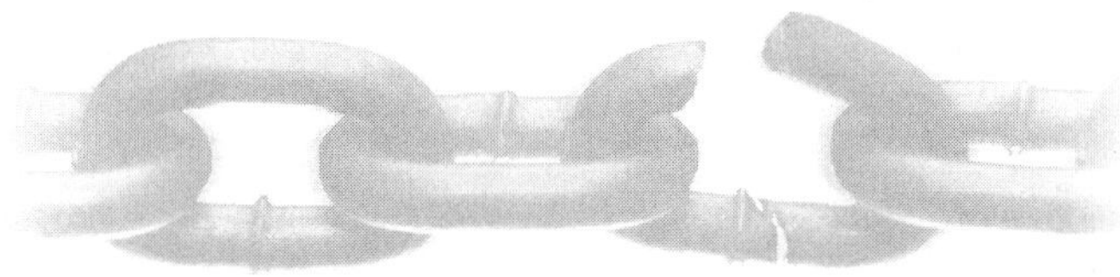

Walking after the Spirit is power to walk through life.

Step out in faith each morning with your head held high!

DAY

32

MERCY

...I am in deep distress. Let us fall into the hands of the Lord, for His mercy is great; but do not let me fall into the hands of men (2 Samuel 24:14 NIV).

REFLECTION

Mercy says, "God, I know he was disobedient; I know he didn't do what You told him to, but can You find it in Your heart to show him just a little mercy? After all, Daddy, he is Your child and You know he really loves You. To the best of his human frailty he does try to obey You and serve You. So if You would (and I know because of Your goodness You can), will You please forgive him and show him Your mercy? Not just some mercy, or any mercy, but *Your* mercy."

God's mercy is not like any kind of mercy. You cannot possibly compare God's mercy with man's mercy because God's mercy is not based on the condition of what we've done. It is based on what God has done through the shed blood of Jesus Christ. It is through the blood of Jesus Christ that we have redemption of our sins. Our goody-two-shoes behavior doesn't count. So now we're truly liberated because we no longer have to worry about being good enough. We are accepted and beloved of the Father. Now that's something to shout about!

Man's mercy is a different case. Man's mercy is based upon your ability to redeem yourself and change your wicked ways. God's mercy and forgiveness are based on His will to redeem you and His ability to empower you with His Spirit to transform you from your wicked ways. Man is inconsistent. God is consistent. Man is wishy-washy. God is stable. Man is flaky and, most of the time, helpless. God is wonderful and—all of the time—able.

(POWER FOR LIVING, CHAPTER 9)

Power Living Perspective

1. How well do you know God's mercy? Are you confident that mercy is speaking on your behalf to God Almighty?

2. How is God's mercy different from people's mercy? Describe three ways.

3. Define *mercy* in no less than 25 words.

4. Why is God so merciful? Are you as merciful as you could be?

5. "Man is inconsistent. God is consistent. Man is wishy-washy. God is stable." List five more contrasts between God and humans.

MEDITATION

O give thanks unto the Lord; for He is good: for His mercy endureth forever (Psalm 136:1).

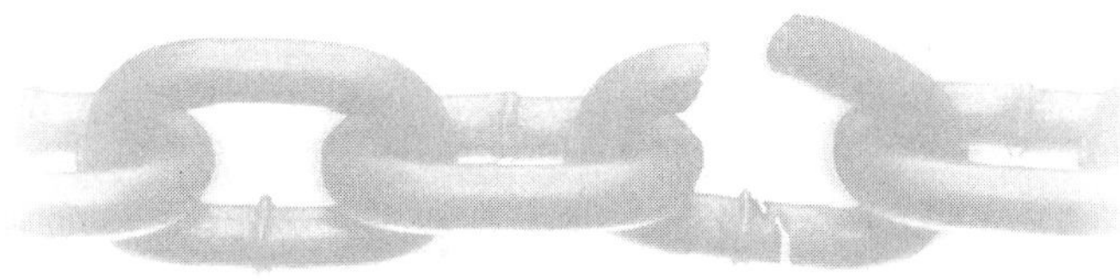

How merciful are you?

DAY
33

Power to Persist and Persevere

Let us draw near with a true heart in full assurance of faith, having our hearts sprinkled from an evil conscience, and our bodies washed with pure water. Let us hold fast the profession of our faith without wavering; (for He is faithful that promised) (Hebrews 10:22-23).

REFLECTION

My brothers and sisters, you may be going through hell right now. The fact of the matter is you must accept the reality that God the Father, Creator of Heaven and earth, is trying to mold you and transform you. God wants to change you into what He has declared as His purpose for your life and that which He spoke about in His written Word. That word is: You are more than a conqueror through Jesus Christ who loves you (see Rom. 8:37). You are the righteousness of God in Christ Jesus (see Rom. 3:22). Greater is He who is in you than he who is in the world (see 1 John 4:4). You have the power to tread upon serpents and scorpions and over all the power of the enemy (see Luke 10:19). No weapon formed against you shall prosper (see Isa. 54:17). You really are the head and not the tail, above and not beneath, the rich and not the poor (see Deut. 28:13).

You, my brothers and sisters, are indeed what God's Word says you are. You are to appropriate what the Word says you are and what the Word says you have. It involves more than just "believing and receiving!"

You've got to be able to persist and move forward in the will of God for your life. Your persistence must continue even when everything seems to be falling apart and when it looks like nothing is turning out right. Stop whining. Learn to stand up under pressure. Set the vision of God before you like a flint and move forward full speed ahead with the plan of God.

(POWER FOR LIVING, Chapter 10)

Power Living Perspective

1. "You are more than a conqueror through Jesus Christ who loves you (see Rom. 8:37)." Write what this means to you personally.

2. "Greater is He who is in you than he who is in the world (see 1 John 4:4)." Write what this means to you personally.

3. "You have the power to tread upon serpents and scorpions and over all the power of the enemy (see Luke 10:19)." Write what this means to you personally.

____

____

____

____

____

____

____

____

4. "No weapon formed against you shall prosper (see Isa. 54:17)." Write what this means to you personally.

____

____

____

____

____

____

____

____

____

5. "You really are the head and not the tail, above and not beneath, the rich and not the poor (see Deut. 28:13)." Write what this means to you personally.

MEDITATION

Because you have kept My command to persevere, I also will keep you from the hour of trial which shall come upon the whole world, to test those who dwell on the earth (Revelation 3:10 NKJV).

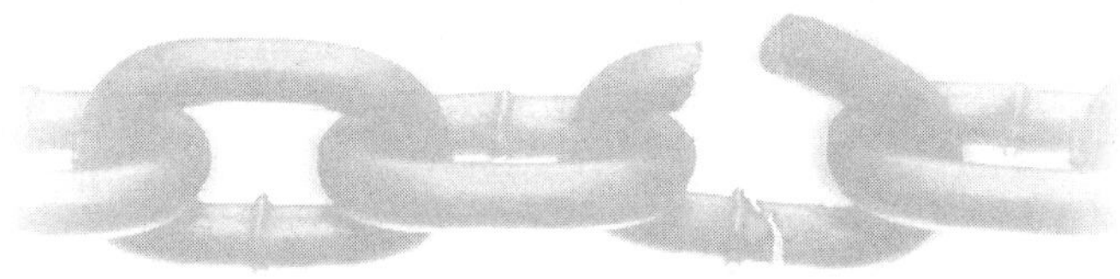

Persist and persevere.

DAY 34

EVEN THOUGH...

Though He slay me, yet will I trust in Him: but I will maintain mine own ways before Him. He also shall be my salvation... (Job 13:15-16).

REFLECTION

The path to true spiritual, moral, physical, and economic success is the road less traveled. It's the straight and narrow road. In order to truly increase, you must first decrease. Before a seed buds and bears fruit it must first fall into the ground and die. In order to gain your life, you must first lose it for Christ's sake. If you really want to know Christ in the power of His resurrection, you must have fellowship with His sufferings. We've got to stop being enemies of the cross. We must take up our cross and bear it daily. The going has always been rough, so we might as well set our minds to get tough. Don't just praise God when everything seems fine and well. We've got to start learning how to cry out to Him in praise even when it appears we're going through hell.

God wants to get you to the point that you become as faithful as the patriarch Job. When anointed people get under pressure, like Job they say, "Even though He slay me yet shall I praise Him." He wants you to differ from the children of Israel, who only murmured and complained when He brought them out of Egyptian bondage. God knows you're anointed, and anointed people have the qualities of Moses, Paul, Stephen, and Jesus. They are faithful, regardless of the afflictions, unto death. In this, God is greatly glorified.

(POWER FOR LIVING, Chapter 10)

POWER LIVING PERSPECTIVE

1. Are your feet walking on the straight and narrow road? Where will it lead you?

2. Do your feet wander off the narrow road unto the wide superhighway of life? Where will it lead you?

3. "We've got to start learning how to cry out to Him in praise even when it appears we're going through hell." Describe a time when you felt overwhelmed with pain. Did you cry out to Him in praise?

4. Are you as faithful as Job? Remember, God only allowed satan to test Job to his limit. Do you believe that you will not be tested beyond your limit?

5. "God knows you're anointed, and anointed people have the qualities of Moses, Paul, Stephen, and Jesus." What qualities do you have that are similar to those of Moses, Paul, Stephen, and Jesus? List them.

MEDITATION

Offer the sacrifices of righteousness, and put your trust in the Lord (Psalm 4:5).

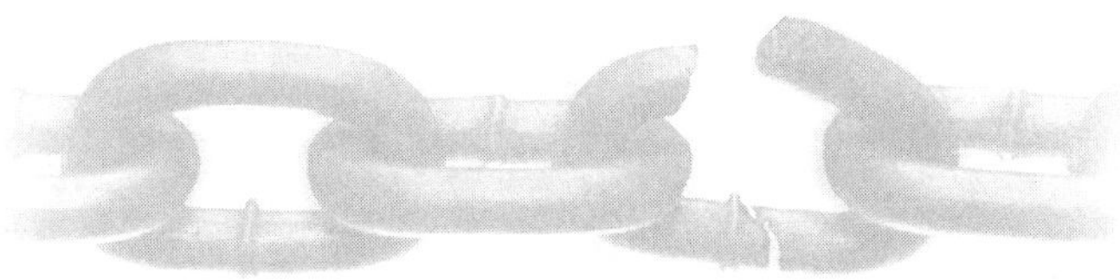

Even though your world may be crashing down around you,
God has given you the power to persist and persevere.

DAY

35

POWER-FILLED DETERMINATION

...This is My beloved Son, in whom I am well pleased (Matthew 3:17).

REFLECTION

There is something about suffering that builds determination in your life. It is power-filled determination that says, "I don't care how you feel about me, what you think about me, or even who's looking at me. When I feel the need or urge to, I'm going to praise the Lord. You may want me to be quiet, calm, and controlled, but I'm going to bless Him anyway. I've been through too much to let somebody bind or hinder me from giving God praise. The Lord has delivered me and seen me through too many unbearable situations. I've had to shed too many tears of heartache and pain to let somebody stop me from giving God the praise and honor that is due only Him. My situation was so bad that only God could have brought me out."

(POWER FOR LIVING, Chapter 10)

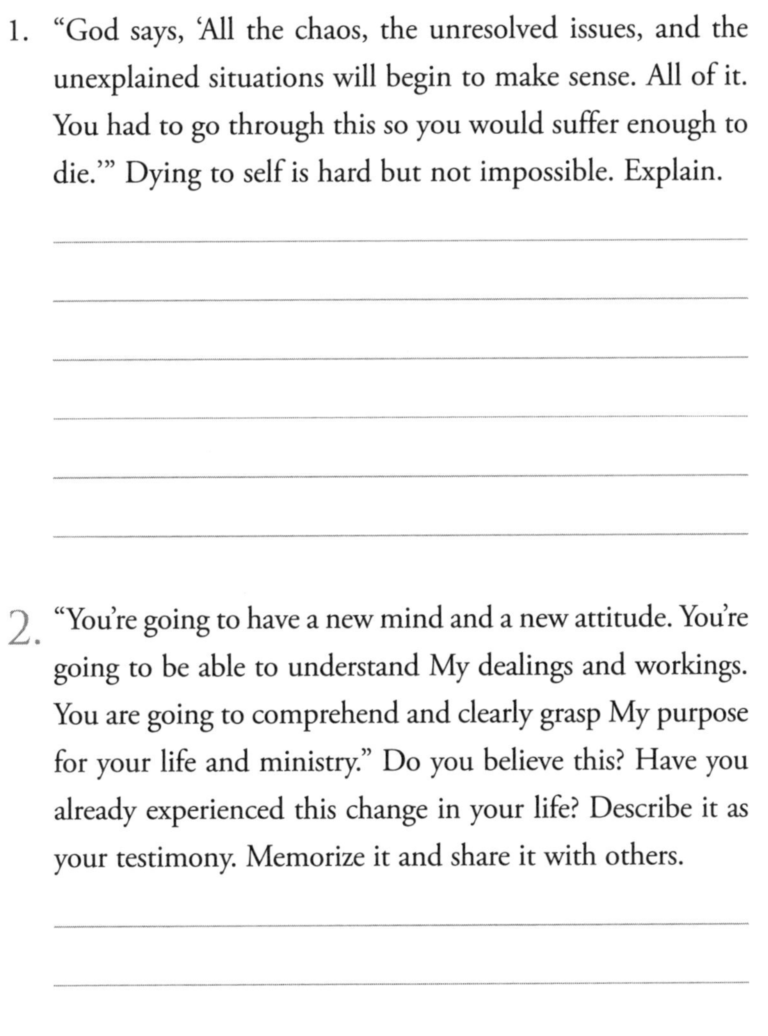

Power Living Perspective

1. "God says, 'All the chaos, the unresolved issues, and the unexplained situations will begin to make sense. All of it. You had to go through this so you would suffer enough to die.'" Dying to self is hard but not impossible. Explain.

2. "You're going to have a new mind and a new attitude. You're going to be able to understand My dealings and workings. You are going to comprehend and clearly grasp My purpose for your life and ministry." Do you believe this? Have you already experienced this change in your life? Describe it as your testimony. Memorize it and share it with others.

3. "God wants to bring you to the point where you will not only be strong when troubles come, but stable. He wants you to stop worrying all the time about the outcome of things." Are you a habitual worrier? Are there certain things that cause you to worry constantly? Children? Work? Finances? Ask God to deliver you from this habit. Trust that He loves your children even more than you do. Trust Him to provide for your needs.

4. "The next time something devastating happens in your life, you need not get upset. You should say, 'I have been through this before. I've been lonely before, I've had to cry before, I've suffered before. I have had to press my way

through before, and I found out that all things work together for good to them who love the Lord and are called according to His purpose.'" Are you prepared to say this and trust Him?

5. "If He has to move a mountain, do a miracle, or create a wonder, I have faith and confidence that my God will do it. If I just continue to persist…." Hope in God is the only true and lasting hope you have in life. Does this thought bring you comfort? Why or why not?

MEDITATION

And not only that, but we also glory in tribulations, knowing that tribulation produces perseverance; and perseverance, character; and character, ***hope****. Now* ***hope does not disappoint****, because the love of God has been poured out in our hearts by the Holy Spirit who was given to us* (Romans 5:3-5 NKJV).

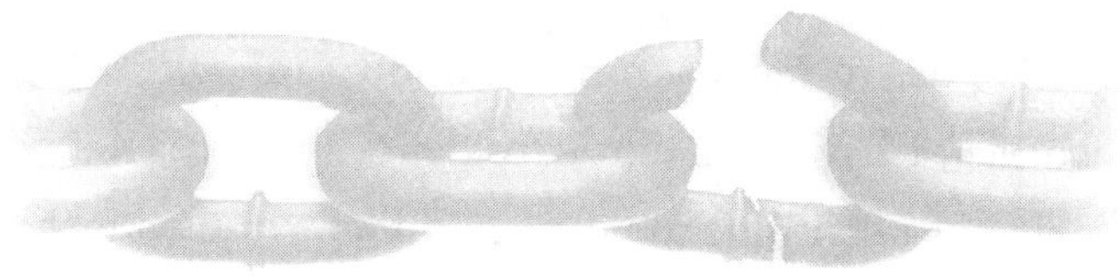

Hope in God does not disappoint!

DAY 36

BE STEADFAST

Therefore, my beloved brethren, be ye stedfast, unmovable, always abounding in the work of the Lord, forasmuch as ye know that your labour is not in vain in the Lord (1 Corinthians 15:58).

REFLECTION

God's Word and Spirit force life into existence. God says, "I'm going to sweeten you up so when you go in the fragrance of My presence, you will fill the entire atmosphere. The place will light up because you walked in."

If you want to be anointed—if you want to receive the power for living—you've got to be crushed. If you want to be anointed, you're going to have to go through some things. Have you been through something? If you really want to be blessed by the anointing, let somebody who has been through something preach, teach, or sing. If you are among all of those who say *hallelujah* just to be saying *hallelujah* because a man or woman of God preaches, you don't have any flavor. All of you who have been beaten, battered, shaken, crushed, rejected, and ostracized have a fragrance coming out of you sweeter than the honey in the honeycomb. It's better than the Rose of Sharon—unto God a sweet-smelling savor in His nostrils. And the more you're afflicted, the more anointed you will become.

(POWER FOR LIVING, Chapter 10)

Power Living Perspective

1. Do you know someone who "lights up the room" with his or her presence? What about that person makes you take notice?

2. How can *you* put on the presence of God so that you light up a room when you enter? Do you think it is possible? Write your feelings.

3. What is your favorite perfume, cologne, or aftershave lotion? How long does the fragrance last—all morning, all day, into the evening? How long does the fragrance of God linger—how far and wide?

4. "All of you who have been beaten, battered, shaken, crushed, rejected, and ostracized have a fragrance coming out of you sweeter than the honey in the honeycomb." Do you believe this? Why or why not?

5. How steadfast are you in God's love? His hope? His mercy? His faithfulness?

MEDITATION

Therefore, my beloved brethren, be steadfast, immovable, always abounding in the work of the Lord, knowing that your labor is not in vain in the Lord (1 Corinthians 15:58 NKJV).

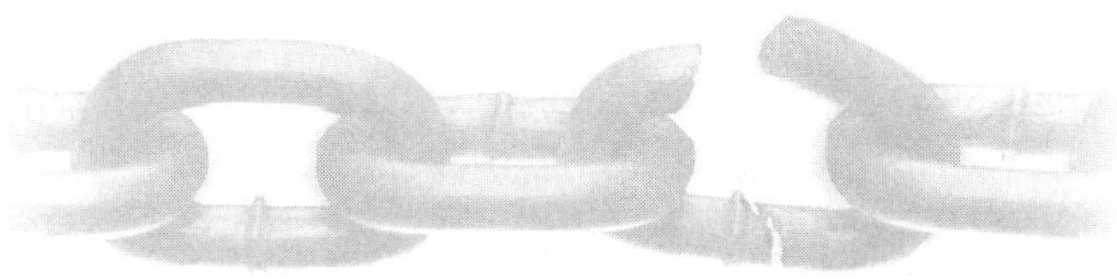

Being steadfast means being constant, steady, firm, stable, unwavering, uniform, enduring. Faith in a steadfast God brings hope and power for living.

DAY 37

Go Forth With Power!

And when they had prayed, the place was shaken where they were assembled together; and they were all filled with the Holy Ghost, and they spake the word of God with boldness (Acts 4:31).

REFLECTION

Peter and John had been in jail for preaching the Gospel and healing a lame man in the name of Jesus. The Bible says that God had been greatly glorified in the hearts of the people as a result of the miracle the Lord had wrought through Peter and John. The rulers of the city sought to punish the apostles for preaching in Jesus' name, but God had come through and performed a miracle on their behalf, granting their release.

Now you know how it is when the Church comes under persecution. Believers come to fellowship service acting real funny! So Brother Peter said to himself, *I better get a good message for this service. Let me pull something here from the Book of Psalms. I'll use the passage when King David was all perplexed and confused, asking the Lord, "Why do the heathen rage?"*

Peter began to preach this message to them about God and purpose. Peter and John had been in jail all night long, had the prints of chains still on their wrists, and had probably been without food or water. Here was a chance to really be downtrodden and discouraged. Instead, Peter, the former "Teacher's pet," started preaching to them about purpose. He began (and I paraphrase): "You know folks, we just had a wonderful experience of God's Spirit as we were partying (celebrating) at the Pentecost festival, and as expected, we ran into a little trouble with the law for jamming (singing and praising) too loud, too hard, and too strong. We experienced a trial that caused us a little bit of pain and discomfort, but you're going to see God turn it around and make it work for your good."

(POWER FOR LIVING, Chapter 11)

POWER LIVING PERSPECTIVE

1. "The Bible says that God had been greatly glorified in the hearts of the people as a result of the miracle the Lord had wrought through Peter and John." Have you witnessed a miracle? Write about it. If not, write about a miracle in the Bible. How did it glorify God?

2. When you are wrongly accused, how do you react? Do you play the role of victim for as long as possible? What can we learn from Peter's message?

3. If God has delivered you from a trial, do you give Him all the glory? Do you thank Him? Do you trust Him to deliver you from the next tribulation?

4. Peter and John had received holy power to speak with boldness. How can you make yourself available to receive the power for living?

5. Describe what you think it was like to hear the "rushing mighty wind" and see the divided tongues of fire upon them. (See Acts 2:1-7.) Have you had a similar experience? Describe it.

MEDITATION

Beloved, think it not strange concerning the fiery trial which is to try you, as though some strange thing happened unto you: ***But rejoice, inasmuch as ye are partakers of Christ's sufferings; that, when His glory shall be revealed, ye may be glad also with exceeding joy.*** *If ye be reproached for the name of Christ, happy are ye; for the Spirit of glory and of God resteth upon you...* (1 Peter 4:12-14).

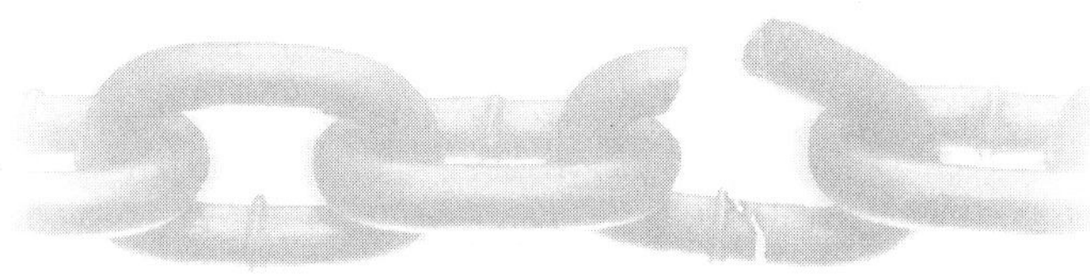

Rejoice!

DAY

38

GROANINGS

Likewise the Spirit also helps in our weaknesses. For we do not know what we should pray for as we ought, but the Spirit Himself makes intercession for us with groanings which cannot be uttered (Romans 8:26 NKJV).

REFLECTION

Sometimes we're confronted with problems and situations that are so complex that they very often go beyond our ability to understand and comprehend. That's exactly why the apostle Paul said, "…the Spirit also helpeth our infirmities: for we know not what we should pray for as we ought: but the Spirit itself maketh intercession for us with groanings which cannot be uttered" (Rom. 8:26). By infirmities, Paul means human weakness that indicates the inability to produce the desired results or fulfill the necessary need. The notation for infirmities in the Ryrie Study Bible, as it relates to Romans 8:26, says that these particular infirmities are "our inability to pray intelligently about 'certain' situations."

Regardless of how well you know the Word, and regardless of how prolific you are at praying and quoting the Word, you've got to know that there will come a time when you will not know what it is that you need in order to rectify a situation in accordance with the will of God. As the saints of God, if we are serious about submitting to and obeying the will of God for our lives, we need to have total reliance upon the Holy Spirit to direct us in all our daily affairs, "…because [the Spirit] maketh intercession for the saints according to the will of God" (Rom. 8:27 ASV).

(POWER FOR LIVING, Chapter 11)

Power Living Perspective

1. "...there will come a time when you will not know what it is that you need in order to rectify a situation in accordance with the will of God." Have you faced this type of situation? Describe how you handled it.

____

____

____

____

____

2. "As the saints of God, if we are serious about submitting to and obeying the will of God for our lives, we need to have total reliance upon the Holy Spirit...." Have you given total control of your prayer life over to the Holy Spirit? What does that mean to you?

____

____

____

____

____

3. How do you think your prayer life will change if the Holy Spirit is in total control?

____

____

____

____

____

____

____

____

4. Speaking with boldness means being confident in what you are saying. Do you feel prepared to share your faith with others? Why or why not? Do you rely on the power of the Holy Spirit?

____

____

____

____

____

____

____

____

5. Believers are to spread the good news of Jesus Christ. Have you been the witness that you think He wants you to be? How can you ignite others when sharing His Word?

MEDITATION

Now He who searches the hearts knows what the mind of the Spirit is, because He makes intercession for the saints according to the will of God (Romans 8:27 NKJV).

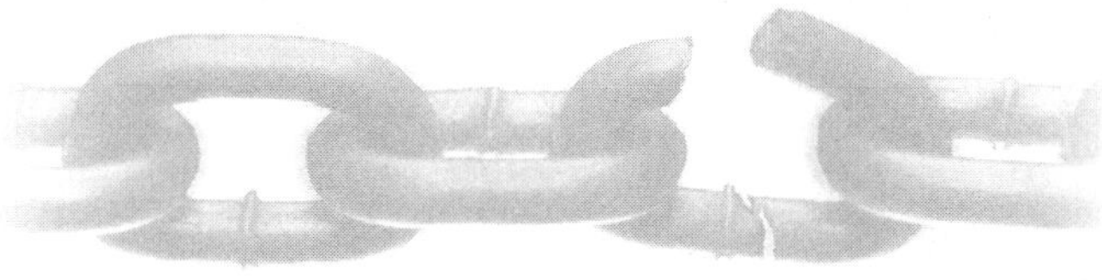

What does your heart reveal to Him who searches?

DAY

39

Filled With the Spirit of God

Who also made us sufficient as ministers of the new covenant, not of the letter but of the Spirit; for the letter kills, but the Spirit gives life (2 Corinthians 3:6 NKJV).

REFLECTION

The disciples prayed and the place where they were assembled began to shake. God filled them with the Holy Ghost and they started speaking the Word with boldness. The basic adherence to the "Word of Faith" doctrine, contrary to all the doomsayers, is a true and authentic biblical principal. However, you can't just speak the Word out of your flesh and expect it to work the will of God for your life. You have got to be, without exception, led of the Spirit in all that you do in God. The Bible says that "the letter [alone] killeth, but the Spirit giveth life" (2 Cor. 3:6). That's what most of the New Testament is—letters. The Word and the Spirit must always be one together, not one without the other. The two must agree.

When the disciples prayed, they were filled with the Spirit of God. "Well," you might say, "I've already been baptized with the Spirit of God. I've already been filled. I even speak with new tongues!" That may be so, but are you filled with His Spirit and His power and glory now? I know you may have been baptized and filled with the Spirit years ago when you first got saved, but are you filled now? If not, He'll fill you again. To everyone and everybody who opens up to Him, God says, "I will fill them." To everybody who says, "I'm thirsty!" God says, "I'll fill them." Anyone whose cry is, "Lord, I'm longing for Your presence," God says, "I'll fill you." God wants to fill you until you get bold, until timid folks get bold, nervous folks get bold, and scared folks get bold. God says, "I'm gonna fill you until you go tell of the grace and goodness of the Lord."

(POWER FOR LIVING, Chapter 11)

POWER LIVING PERSPECTIVE

1. "However, you can't just speak the Word out of your flesh and expect it to work the will of God for your life. You have got to be, without exception, led of the Spirit in all that you do in God." What do these statements mean to you personally?

2. "I know you might have been baptized and filled with the Spirit years ago when you first got saved, but are you filled now? If not, He'll fill you again." Have you asked for a fill-up lately? What's holding you back?

3. "God wants to fill you until you get bold, until timid folks get bold, nervous folks get bold, and scared folks get bold." Are you a naturally timid or non-assertive person? What will it take for you to "get bold"?

4. What is the scariest thing about speaking boldly? How can you overcome that fear?

5. Have you been baptized with the Holy Spirit with the evidence of speaking in tongues? Why or why not? What does this experience mean to you?

MEDITATION

Then Jesus, being filled with the Holy Spirit, returned from the Jordan and was led by the Spirit into the wilderness (Luke 4:1 NKJV).

If Jesus was filled with the Holy Spirit to accomplish His task on earth, how much more we need the Holy Spirit to help us.

DAY
40

SPEAK THE WORD

Thy word is a lamp unto my feet, and a light unto my path (Psalm 119:105).

Reflection

You need to speak the Word of God with boldness, not with your feelings, your problems, or your situations. You need to set your mind on God's promise and God's Word, and begin to speak the Word of God with boldness. We need not let external circumstances and situations dictate our feelings, behavior, and mindset. Stop believing what others say and start believing what the Word of God says. What does the Word say?

God's Word declares, "My God shall supply all my needs according to His riches in glory by Christ Jesus...The Lord is my shepherd and I shall not want...By His stripes I am healed...If any man be in Christ he is a new creature, old things have passed away, all things have become new...The earth is the Lord's and the fullness thereof, and they that dwell therein" (see Phil. 4:19; Ps. 23:1; Isa. 53:5; 2 Cor. 5:17; Ps. 24:1). Speak the Word; speak the Word! If the Word said you shall have whatever you say, then you shall have whatever you say. I dare you to say it.

(POWER FOR LIVING, Chapter 11)

Power Living Perspective

1. "My God shall supply all my needs according to His riches in glory by Christ Jesus." Do you believe this? Why?

2. "The Lord is my shepherd and I shall not want." Do you believe this? Why?

3. "By His stripes I am healed." Do you believe this? Why?

4. "If any man be in Christ he is a new creature, old things have passed away, all things have become new." Do you believe this? Why?

5. "The earth is the Lord's and the fullness thereof, and they that dwell therein." Do you believe this? Why?

MEDITATION

For the word of God is ***living*** *and* ***powerful****, and sharper than any two-edged sword, piercing even to the division of soul and spirit, and of joints and marrow, and is a discerner of the thoughts and intents of the heart* (Hebrews 4:12 NKJV).

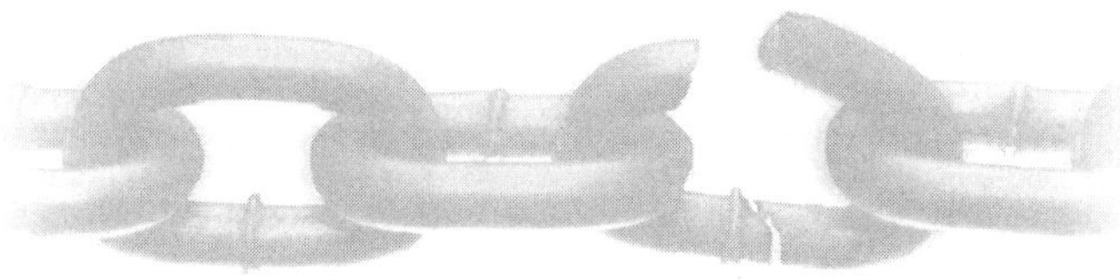

Your strongest defense is the Word of God.

Additional Notes

Additional copies of this book and other book titles from DESTINY IMAGE are available at your local bookstore.

Call toll-free: 1-800-722-6774.

Send a request for a catalog to:

Destiny Image® Publishers, Inc.
P.O. Box 310
Shippensburg, PA 17257-0310

"Speaking to the Purposes of God for This Generation and for the Generations to Come."

For a complete list of our titles, visit us at www.destinyimage.com.